D1279440

From the Editors of Voyageur Press

# *Majestic* WHITETAILS

Voyageur Press

Text copyright © 1997 by Voyageur Press
Photographs copyright © 1997 by the photographers noted

All rights reserved. No part of this work may be reproduced or used in any form by any means—graphic, electronic, or mechanical, including photocopying, recording, taping, or any information storage and retrieval system—without written permission of the publisher.

Edited by Michael Dregni and Todd R. Berger
Designed by Andrea Rud
Printed in China

97 98 99 00 01 5 4 3 2 1

Library of Congress Cataloging-in-Publication Data
Majestic whitetails / from the editors of Voyageur Press ;
   [edited by Michael Dregni and Todd R. Berger].
        p.   cm.
     ISBN 0-89658-337-6
     1. White-tailed deer hunting.  2. Hunting stories.
I. Dregni, Michael, 1961-    . II. Berger, Todd R.
III. Voyageur Press.
SK301.M33   1997
799.2'7652—dc21                    97-424
                         CIP

Published by Voyageur Press, Inc.
123 North Second Street, P.O. Box 338
Stillwater, MN 55082 U.S.A.
612-430-2210, fax 612-430-2211

Distributed in Canada by Raincoast Books
8680 Cambie Street, Vancouver, B.C. V6P 6M9

*Educators, fundraisers, premium and gift buyers, publicists, and marketing managers:* Looking for creative products and new sales ideas? Voyageur Press books are available at special discounts when purchased in quantities, and special editions can be created to your specifications. For details contact the marketing department.

**Permissions**
"Me, The Mighty Buckhunter" from *Iron River, My Home Town* by Fred P. Lund. Copyright © 1975 by Fred P. Lund. Reprinted by permission of Anita Lund, 2267 East Shawnee Drive, North St. Paul, MN 55109.
"The Hunting Lesson" from *The Grasshopper Trap* by Patrick F. McManus. Copyright © 1985 by Patrick F. McManus. Reprinted by permission of Henry Holt and Co., Inc.
"The Test of a Deer Stand" from *Learning Nature by a Country Road* by Tom Anderson. Copyright © 1989 by Tom Anderson. Reprinted by permission of Tom Anderson and Voyageur Press, Inc.
"You've Got to Suffer!" by Gordon MacQuarrie. Copyright © 1967 by Gordon MacQuarrie. Reprinted by permission of Game & Fish Publications, Inc.
"Mister Howard Was a Real Gent" from *The Old Man and the Boy* by Robert Ruark. Copyright © 1953, 1954, 1955, 1956, 1957 by Robert C. Ruark. Copyright © 1985 by Harold Matson, Paul Gitlin, and Chemical Bank. Reprinted by permission of Henry Holt and Co., Inc.
"Swamp Buck" from *Is She Coming Too? Memoirs of a Lady Hunter* by Frances Hamerstrom. Copyright © 1989 by Frances Hamerstrom. Reprinted by permission of Iowa State University Press.
"Stag Pants Galahads" from *The Collected Works of Sigurd F. Olson: The Early Writings: 1921–1934* by Sigurd F. Olson. Copyright © 1988. Reprinted by permission of Voyageur Press, Inc.
"Race at Morning" from *Big Woods* by William Faulkner. Copyright © 1931, 1940, 1942, 1951, 1955 by William Faulkner. Reprinted by permission of Random House, Inc.
"Life in Wisconsin's Old-Time Deer Camps" by Mel Ellis. Copyright © 1978 by Mel Ellis. Reprinted by permission of Larry Sternig/Jack Byrne Agency.

Page 1: *A whitetail buck in autumn grass. (Photo © Robert McKemie/EarthImages)*
Page 2: *A whitetail buck hurdles a barbed-wire fence. (Photo © Denver Bryan)*
Page 3, inset: *A successful deer hunt near Walker, Minnesota, in the early 1930s. (Collection of Robert J. Hohman)*
Facing page: *A majestic ten-point buck. (Photo © Bruce Montagne)*
Page 6: *A dropped whitetail antler layered in ice. (Photo © Michael H. Francis)*

# CONTENTS

Introduction

# MAJESTIC WHITETAILS

Hanging on the wall above the fireplace, a trophy whitetail with a magnificent rack of antlers is a symbol of the majesty of the whitetailed deer and evidence of a successful hunt. But this is only one side of the story. The trophy also recalls things past, a mnemonic that summons up the story behind the trophy and the atmosphere of autumn days in the field. The legend is usually just waiting to be put into spoken word, impatient on the tip of the hunter's tongue, prepared to come tumbling forth like a waterfall at a casual inquiry as to the trophy's origin. The hunter may hide behind a mask of modesty and feign deep reluctance to recount the momentous event, but ultimately the dilemma is not in getting the hunter to tell the tale. It is in getting the storyteller to stop the oration once begun.

The seasoned outdoorsman and humorist Patrick F. McManus noted that exaggeration and hunting stories often become inexplicably intertwined. In his 1981 confessional story "My First Deer, and Welcome to It" from the book *They Shoot Canoes, Don't They?*, McManus astutely observed, "For a first deer, there is no habitat so lush and fine as a hunter's memory. Three decades and more of observation have convinced me that a first deer not only lives on in the memory of a hunter but thrives there, increasing in points and pounds with each passing year until at last it reaches full maturity, which is to say, big enough to shade a team of Belgian draft horses in its shadow at high noon." McManus then recounts the story of his first deer, hand over his heart and swearing on a stack of bibles to the veracity of his tall tale.

*An alert Texas whitetail buck. (Photo © Len Rue, Jr.)*

Stories of that first deer—as well as of all the others that follow—may have a healthy dose of exclamation points, superlatives, and adjectives added to stretch the truth like a rubber band. But do not cast too heavy a load of blame on the hunter-turned-storyteller, as exaggeration may only be an unkind word for colorful storytelling. In the end, the whitetailed deer mounted on the wall satisfies the burden of proof.

*Majestic Whitetails* is a collection of whitetail hunting tales by master storytellers. The stories come from a variety of writers, some of whom bear more renown for their skill with a rifle than with a pen, while another won the Nobel Prize for Literature and has only colorful hunting stories to prove his prowess as a stalker of deer. The writers include well-known authors Patrick McManus, Robert Ruark, Gordon MacQuarrie, William Faulkner, and Sigurd F. Olson. Also included are stories by three writers who may be less famous but have great tales to tell: Mel Ellis, Fred P. Lund, and Tom Anderson.

*Majestic Whitetails* is also an album of spectacular deer photography from several of today's leading whitetail photographers. The images come from all over the United States and Canada and encompass a virtual "Who's Who" of nature photographers, including Erwin and Peggy Bauer, Steve Bentsen, Denver Bryan, Jeanne Drake, Michael H. Francis, D. Robert Franz, Henry H. Holdsworth, Jerry and Barbara Jividen, Stephen Kirkpatrick, Ann Littlejohn, Doug Locke, Thomas Mangelsen, Bill Marchel, Robert McKemie, Bruce Montagne, Gregory M. Nelson, Leonard Lee Rue III, Jamie Ruggles, Chica Stracener, Tom Urban, and Art Wolfe. Quite simply, this is some of the best whitetail photography ever to appear in print.

In choosing these stories and photographs, the difficulty was not in finding a sampling of good material but in finding a place to stop. We hope this collection satisfies you, evoking the thrill of the hunt on those evenings sitting by the hearth during the long stretch between hunting seasons.

*Dominated by a huge, attentive buck, a whitetail herd is wary for any sign of danger. (Photo © Jeanne Drake, Las Vegas, NV)*

Chapter 1

---

# THE
# FIRST DEER

There were those times when I was a kid, hunting and trapping and
sometimes spending several days and nights alone in the woods, when I'd
have a flash of insight that was usually gone as swiftly as it came—the
vaguest feeling of how aboriginal hunters must feel, and what real hunting,
pure-quill, honest-to-God real hunting, is all about. One strong flash of this
to a boy—one swift heady taste of this utter wild freedom and perception—
is enough to keep him hunting all his days. Not just for meat or horns,
but hunting for that flash of insight again, trying to close the magic
circle of man, wilderness and deer.

—John Madson, Foreword to The Deer Book, 1980

# ME, THE MIGHTY BUCKHUNTER

## by Fred P. Lund

In his youth, the future buckhunter Fred Lund was known as "Wiggles" by his family, including his father, who was an astute deer hunter in his own right. The Lund family hunted whitetails at their deer hunting camp, known affectionately as the Homestead. The camp was near Iron River in the far northern reaches of Wisconsin, not too far from the city of Superior and a stone's throw from the great lake by the same name. Wisconsin has always been whitetail country, a land in which a young boy often comes of age pursuing the elusive deer. Wiggles Lund was justly proud of his first—and second—whitetail bucks.

This story first appeared in 1975 in Lund's self-published book of autobiographical sketches, *Iron River, My Home Town*. Lund was prolific in recording and sharing his memories, including many deer-hunting tales; his other self-published books include *I Mind: Memories of the Old Hunting Camp Days* (1969) as well as *And That's The Way It Was* (1973).

Among the many happy memories that I have of my youth, the annual deer hunting season should probably be rated as the greatest event of them all.

Our hunting camp was my grandfather's original homestead about nine miles south of town. We had 160 acres with the nearest farm "of sorts" or another hunting camp miles away. It was a two-story log cabin about 16x24 feet with a "shanty" kitchen tacked on and a front porch that tilted towards "Medicine Bow." There was also a back porch that had a closed-in meat room and woodshed combination and this was also attached to the kitchen. Behind the kitchen and wired to the eaves was a wooden triangular trough that brought the rainwater into a large wooden barrel on the northwest corner.

It was located in a large valley that was open at one end, "like a broken saucer," according to my father's description. There was about an acre of cleared land around the buildings and each year we plowed about a dozen furrows around the field because of the danger of forest fires. There was a small log barn which was the original dwelling on the east slope of the

Page 13–14: *A buck searches for food after an early morning snowfall. (Photo © Gregory M. Nelson)*
Page 14, inset: *It's obvious here who bagged his first deer. This photograph was taken near Phillips, Wisconsin, circa 1900. (Photo by S. A. Johnson, courtesy Minnesota Historical Society)*
Facing page: *A classic deer-hunting rifle: the Winchester Model 1894 .25/35 caliber, pictured with antique Coleman camping gear. (Photo © William W. Headrick)*

clearing, a root cellar dug in the north side hill, and the "outside plumbing," which was often called "The Cabin in the Pines."

The pump, located in the lowest part of the valley, produced wonderful, clear, cold water from 98 feet down and it took that many strokes of the pump handle to bring it up. The filling of two 14-quart galvanized pails was a good "meal settler," so my father always told me.

I remember the "homestead" as a rather barren spot. There was some scrub oak, second growth "popple," a few birch, soft maple, and wild pin cherry trees growing on the hills. The entire valley seemed to have plenty of blackened stumps, pocket gopher mounds, and an abundance of sweet fern closing in on the thin, wild hay. The soil was sandy and after the timber had been cut the soil must have felt that it had produced what the Lord had meant it to produce, so it settled back to making no effort at beautifying the surroundings.

The inside of the cabin was well furnished. Many of the beds, dishes, and cooking utensils came from my grandfather's hotel, which he had started the day after Iron River burned in 1892, and some other things came from the logging camps around the area. Also it seemed that many people gave us things that were "just right for the hunting camp." Most of all it was filled with countless wonderful memories.

This was a rather unique hunting camp because for many years our entire family moved out there lock, stock, and barrel. It was my father's vacation, but it meant quite a workout for my mother as she did the cooking for many years as well as kept the place in order, and even with help, that was no small assignment as we often had 15 or 20 hunters besides our family.

I suppose that I was nine or ten when I struck out on my own as a pursuer of the mighty whitetail. After I had finished my assigned chores in the morning I was on my own, and the entrancing wilderness of cut-over timberland beckoned to me.

In those days my trusty weapon was a pump action Daisy air rifle that held 50 shots. The previous winter I had found a 20 dollar bill on my way home from school. I came bursting into the house to tell the folks of my good fortune and they were, of course, happy that I had suddenly become rich, but they also explained to me that the money wasn't really mine. It had to belong to someone and perhaps the party who had lost it needed it badly. I was finally convinced that the only honest thing to do was to wait and see if anyone put a notice in the local paper. If no one did, my dad promised me that I could have the air rifle that I had been tormenting him to buy for me.

I can't remember how long I had to wait, but finally one day when I stopped in the printing office where my dad had his office he said, "Well me bye, let's order that rifle."

By the time he had his coat on, I was already at the Iron River Hardware, which was a block away. I stood inside of the door waiting impatiently for him.

This was a big moment in my life and when I saw him stop and talk to Pete Peterson in the middle of the street, I thought the world would come to an end before he got through. Finally he walked in the door, stamped his feet to clean off the snow, and in his usual manner shouted, "HELLO!"

My father was not a quiet man and when he said hello he wanted everyone to hear it and return the greeting. Ed Bousley, who was standing on a stepladder replacing one of the many drawers on the rack behind the counter, nearly lost his balance and he said as he climbed down, "Gawd damn it, Hakon, you nearly scared the wits out of me."

Dad laughed and told him what we wanted and Ed got out the catalogue.

Youth has no patience and it seemed to me that Ed Bousley was the slowest man in the world as he thumbed through the index and finally came to the "R's." He traced his finger slowly down the column —Revolvers, Rim Locks, Rings, Harness, Rifle Cases, Rifles, "Here it is Hakon, Rifles, Air."

He found page 479, turned the catalogue around and placed it on the counter between us. There were two full pages of BB guns and Dad said, "Pick out the one that you want."

I already knew which one that was and naturally it was the most expensive. Some of the other kids in town had BB guns and I had spent many hours poring over the gun section in the mail order catalogues.

I certainly wasn't going to settle for the single shot and the guns that held 500 or 1000 shots were noisy. The chamber for holding the BBs was in the

*During the rut, a fine buck surveys his snow-covered surroundings. (Photo © Len Rue, Jr.)*

barrel and any movement caused them to shake back and forth. When you become a great game hunter, silence is essential while traversing the forest.

Without any hesitation I put my finger on the illustration of the Daisy Repeating Air Rifle with Pump Action. I knew the description by heart: One of the best known and dependable air rifles made. Metal parts are blued finish and with genuine walnut stock. Has adjustable rear sight and stationary blade front sight. Holds 50 BB air rifle shot in magazine. Length overall, 38 inches. Weight 3¼ pounds. Price $4.48.

I looked up at my father and said, "I want this one, Pa."

I think that he was a little surprised but all he said was, "You know that one only holds 50 shots and it looks like it might be a little long for you." I didn't budge and in two weeks it arrived. In the meantime, I don't suppose that I made over 10 or 12 trips to the hardware store to inquire about it.

The adventure books about Davy Crockett, Daniel Boone, Kit Carson, and Buffalo Bill as well as the stories about the Pawnee, Blackfeet, and Sioux Indians, influenced my early hunting career. It wasn't hard for a ten-year-old with any kind of an imagination to assume the role of one of those great scouts of the frontier or to even wear the moccasins of Sitting Bull or Crazy Horse while venturing out on the well-beaten trails around our hunting camp.

Naturally my hunting apparel had to be similar to my book heroes and although I could not duplicate the buckskin hunting shirt, trousers, or the coonskin cap authentically, there was plenty of khaki cloth around the house. World War I was not too far in the past and it had been very patriotic to wear the color of the uniform of our doughboys "over there," so we had plenty of old shirts and trousers hanging in our back shed.

Daniel Boone always had fringes on his shirt and trousers and of course his rifle was covered with buckskin and it was also fringed. Any kid knew that he did this to keep his rifle from rusting and to camouflage it in the woods, so I did the same.

My brother King, who was only 18 months older than I was but who was far advanced in his thinking and actions, had often acted as the guide and the domineering big brother until I became the proud possessor of my new shootin' iron. From that time on, I became an independent hunter. I would watch until he had left the cabin and then I would take off in the opposite direction.

As I ventured out on one of the three trails that led from the valley, I walked normally, but when I was sure that I was out of sight I assumed the actions of the Indian scout or one of my white heroes. I would place one foot directly ahead of the other in Indian fashion and stop every 20 or 30 feet and crouch to look over the countryside. By following this procedure, the game would not be frightened and anyone who came on my tracks would know that an Indian or a great scout had passed by.

As I progressed along the trails, I very often sighted game. Sometimes it was a red squirrel, on occasion I would spot a partridge, and once it was a weasel who was darting across the crusted snow. As I watched his black tipped tail flicking back and forth, I was so fascinated that I almost forgot to shoot.

Every time I shot at them I knew that I was breaking the code of the deer hunting fraternity, at least at our camp. I had heard my father's final reminder so many times when the men were starting out on a drive, "Remember to look for horns before you shoot and the only critters that are blessed with them in this country are deer. Bear that in mind."

Any hole in the ground not too far from the trail was always worth investigation and my conclusions concerning the inhabitants of the den were based on two things. If it was near the top of a hill it was a wolf and it had to be a badger if it was on lower ground or in a cut bank. In my wonderland of big game there was no such animal as a woodchuck. These detours in my quest for deer captivated me quite often, but the quarry of my dreams was always an eight- or ten-point buck.

Sometimes I would come across a deer trail and there would be fresh tracks. When this happened I would venture off the trail and walk into the woods for 10 or 15 yards fully confident that I would see a buck with a huge rack the size of a rocking chair ambling along.

Always, in my imagination, I would shoot for his eyes so as to blind him and then he would either charge into a large tree and knock himself unconscious or his horns would become entangled in the brush so that he couldn't move. At this point I would

*Having already dropped their antlers, two whitetail bucks do battle with their front feet on river ice. (Photo © Bill Marchel)*

drop my rifle, grab my bowie knife from my belt (one of the butcher knives that I had sneaked out of the kitchen when my mother wasn't looking), and plunge it into his heart again and again until he fell over dead.

In my dreams, I never cleaned him out. In the first place, I wouldn't have known where to begin and there was nothing heroic about this part of the adventure so I conveniently skipped over it and continued the fantasy to my arrival at the hunting camp. All of the hunters would be sitting in the front room when I would triumphantly arrive carrying the heart and liver on a forked branch. Naturally everyone would be astonished and I would be the hero of the day. There would be handshakes, slaps on the back, and many complimentary things said about my skill as a hunter.

Eventually I achieved the next step in big game hunting. When my father felt that King was old enough to use the family shotgun, I graduated to the "Gamegetter." This was an over and under gun that had a skeleton shoulder stock and could be used as a hand gun or rifle. It had an adjustable hammer and the upper barrel held a .22 shell and the lower, a .44. The barrel was only 12 inches long. It was a nice little weapon and as it shot live ammunition, it out-ranked the Daisy in my estimation.

This firearm put an end to the fantastic dreams of shooting a deer with a BB gun, which I knew were impossible anyway but it had been fun. Now there were real stories that I had heard told by the hunters in camp about this one or that one who had killed a deer with a .22. So what if Oscar Nordquist had to shoot his first deer sixteen times with his Stevens

.22? I knew that I could shoot much more accurately than that and I would certainly wait until Mr. Buck got close enough so that I could knock him down with one well-placed shot to the heart or in the head instead of just blazing away like a crazy man, as the story went.

Now I went farther away from the camp and sometimes I even wandered off the trails and cut cross country to prove that I had become a seasoned hunter. I always had a fresh red squirrel tail protruding from a button hole of my coat or in my stocking cap. Once in awhile a snow shoe rabbit fell as my prey and twice that I can remember, I battled and won over porcupines.

My ascension into the realm of the great buckhunters came about in a rather unexpected way. It was not that I wasn't qualified—after all, I was 12 years old and I had been born and raised in the wilds of northern Wisconsin. I had experienced many hunting seasons, I was a second class Boy Scout, and there wasn't a foot of the forest back of our house in town that I wasn't acquainted with. By this time I had snared rabbits, shot woodchucks, and trapped pocket gophers. I knew how to build a teepee and I had helped to skin out many deer. My father had taught me how to handle firearms, I had been allowed to shoot his shotgun as a reward for "bird-dogging" when I accompanied him and my Uncle Pete on partridge hunts, and I had even shot and killed a wounded doe the year before.

Up to this time, however, I had never made the "big time" and I was quite flabbergasted at the way it came about.

In all of the years of hunting at our camp it was the custom of the men to come in for the noon meal. After dinner my dad would take "forty winks" and of course everyone else did the same if they were so inclined. If not, they waited for the afternoon drive until he awakened and was ready to leave.

On that particular day, three of the men had gone into town to take care of some business, two more had gone over to Happles' Lake to bring in a deer that had been shot the day before, and my Uncle Pete Savage had gone out to do a little Indian hunting on his own.

When Dad awakened, Ping Hobbs, who was one of the regulars, approached him with a plan that the remaining three men had been talking over. "Hakon," he said, "what would you think of making that drive from the Nordquist road west of the Camp 20 grade and north to that big opening? Every track this morning was headed that way and I'll bet there are deer in there."

My dad never jumped into anything very fast so after he drank his coffee he said, "I was kind of saving that drive for tomorrow morning when we have a full crew. If those deer are in there, they will still be there tomorrow morning. I was thinking that we could post two men on the Pettingill road and make that Rye Patch drive this afternoon."

Ping had hunted at our camp for a number of years and he knew my dad quite well. It wasn't very often that anyone questioned him about his judgment or plan for a drive, but he was determined that he was going to convince him of the merits of this one.

Dad thought it over for a few minutes and then he said, "But damnit man, we've only got four men. One man can't cover that opening and we'll just chase the deer out and lose a good drive in the morning.

Ping was adamant so he replied, "Hells Bells, Hakon, we've got the kid here. Let's put him in the middle. That will give us three drivers and two standers. He knows how to handle a rifle and I know he can shoot, because if you remember he knocked that doe in the head that you sent me to put out of her misery at Crooked Lake last year "

"Yah," my dad said, "I suppose we could take him along." He looked me over to see if I had suddenly grown any in the last hour.

"Wow!" thought I. This was something that I hadn't even dreamed of. To become one of the regulars was beyond my wildest aspirations. To go along on an actual drive and to carry a rifle was more than I could even comprehend. What's more, the firearm was to be my oldest brother Loche's 30-30 carbine. The thought of carrying this rifle on a deer hunting drive was more than I could believe.

Dad took me to the spot where I was supposed to start on the drive. He made sure that I understood the lay of land and then he said, "Now you walk slow and stop every once in awhile. Keep the wind on the back of your neck and you'll be going the right way. Keep your eyes peeled and don't veer off this deer

*With its wide, tall rack of antlers still coated in velvet, a mature Texas buck watches for danger. (Photo © Steve Bentsen)*

trail. Uncle Miller will be on your right and Leland will be on your left. You'll be able to see them every once in awhile. This deer run will take you straight to the big opening. When you see the opening, stop until you see Ping. I'll be on the Camp 20 grade. Wait until Leland whistles before you start. Good luck and remember to aim."

I could hardly wait until I heard Sag's whistle. Of course I didn't expect to see anything because with my vast knowledge and experience I was sure that the purpose of the driver was to scare the deer to the standers.

Nevertheless I was overjoyed at my sudden promotion to manhood and before I had gone ten yards I was already preparing my story of the hunt—to be told to the kids in school. I had heard so many every evening at the camp and so I would start my story by saying, "One time when we were making the Camp 20 drive. . . ."

It was easy to follow the trail and even though I had to veer to the right or left occasionally when I came to a windfall that the deer had jumped, I always got back on it and the walking was easy.

I had stopped to watch a porcupine as he made his way up a green popple and I was tempted to shoot him but I knew better. This would not only bring the wrath of the other hunters down on me, but it would spoil the drive and I knew that it would be the end of my deer hunting. Such stupid things were not tolerated at Hakon Lund's camp by anyone.

It was near the end of the drive and as I stood daydreaming it happened. The sharp crack of a limb brought me to my senses and I whirled in the direction from which it came. He was coming easy from my right on another run and I knew that he would pass right in front of me because as yet he hadn't seen me.

I don't know which one of us was more startled but when he was directly in front of me and looked my way, I pulled the trigger. As he took off, I ejected the shell and shot again.

It was impossible to miss and I let out a "Whoop!"

What a magnificent buck he was and what a rack! He would go 200 pounds or better. The only

*With the rut in full swing, this prime Florida buck is on the prowl for does. (Photo © Chica Stracener)*

problem was I couldn't find him and I was still jumping around and running pell mell through the trees and back to the place where I had shot when my father came over.

I tried to describe the incident but I was so excited that I couldn't even talk straight. He stood for a minute trying to understand what I was saying and then very calmly he said, "Now wait a minute, boy. Let's start back to where you saw the buck. Where were you and where was he?"

In the meantime Ping had come over and so I reconstructed the happening. They had me go over it step by step. They had heard me shoot both times so finally Ping said, "Where were you when you shot the first time and where was the buck? "

I showed them and described it, "He was coming from my right and just as he got even with me and in front of that big pine, I shot. He kind of crouched so I know I hit him but then to make sure, I shot again." I had heard many stories about a deer flinching and pulling down his flag when he was hit. I hadn't noticed whether his flag dropped but I vividly remembered the fusillade of buck shot that he discharged as he turned the corner and started north.

They could see the fresh tracks and droppings so they knew that I hadn't had a pipe dream. Ping got down on his knees by the tree and looked for blood and then he followed the trail for a few yards. When he came back and stood where I had shot he said, "Damnit, I don't see how you could have missed him at twenty feet. Did you aim?"

"Sure, I aimed," I replied. "I shot for his left shoulder and he's got to be dead."

He stood looking at the pine and I suppose because he had heard stories, he had seen, and he had probably experienced a little buck fever himself, he looked upwards.

I was watching him and when he half laughed and grunted at the same time, I could have died from shame. Pointing to the tree ten feet above the ground he said, "There's the buck, Hakon." Dad looked up at the large branch that was freshly severed and hanging by a shred. He said, "Well don't that beat all. At least you were aiming in the right direction. Don't feel bad, there'll be more."

I wanted to die, I was on the verge of crying, and I was ready to run for camp when Ping said, "Prob-

ably you nicked him on the second shot and he was going so fast that he didn't start to bleed until he was over the hill. I'll bet he's lying down in that stand of jacks this side of the big opening."

What words of comfort to a 12-year-old. I didn't really believe him but I was certainly grateful for his kind words. For years I had a four-horse team of nightmares about that incident and every time I would wake up, I was able to go back to sleep when I thought of what he said. Twenty years later I thanked him!

I was sure that I was going to be kidded and razzed about my stupidity when the story was told that night at camp. As we resumed the drive I could visualize the men sitting around the Round Oak heater laughing and slapping their legs when the climax of the story would be reached and Ping would describe how he had pointed out the severed branch. What I didn't realize at my tender age was that grown men do not make sport of a kid who gets buck fever on his first deer hunting trip.

Believe it or not, we got the buck and he was right where Ping said he would be, but he wasn't lying down when my cousin Sag nailed him. He was going like the hammers of hell for Lake Superior at thirty-foot jumps and he turned a complete somersault when he was hit. Again I was grateful to Ping as he turned him over two or three times to see if I had hit him. I'm sure he wanted to find a tuft of hair that was missing or at least a crease to restore my confidence, but he was as clean as a whistle.

It wasn't until I was 14 that I had my next chance at a buck. My Uncle Pete Savage was returning to camp one evening just as it was getting dark. He had a habit of singing or whistling and on this particular night, as had happened many times before, a buck had appeared on the scene. He had wounded him and trailed him for awhile, but when it became too dark to see he had given up and returned to camp.

After he had told the story that night it was decided that the first drive in the morning would be made in the direction the deer had gone. Everyone was sure that he would be lying down and Uncle Pete was confident that he would be able to find his tracks and we would have another fine buck hanging on the deer rack before noon.

My brother Loche had come home from college

*Their antlers rattling as they strike, whitetail bucks spar with each other on a cold winter day. (Photos © Len Rue, Jr.)*

for the weekend so on this Saturday morning I was demoted. I had been using his 30-30 carbine and I loved it. It was the same type that was carried by the Royal Northwest Mounted Police and it had a ring on the side of the chamber so that the leather saddle thong could be attached to it. As I carried it in the woods I could visualize the Mounties in their scarlet tunics and campaign hats riding out in the wilderness "to get their man." When you are 14 years old, and you have read as many books about the colorful corps as the Iron River Library had on the shelves, plus all of the movies about them shown at Daniels' Theatre, you would be perturbed, too, when your father announced, "Well, Wiggles, it's a good thing that I bought an extra box of shotgun slugs because I have an idea that you will be busy today."

Before we left that morning he could see that I was very unhappy. After all, how low can a man sink when he has to resort to using a shotgun to hunt bucks. I not only felt disgraced but I voiced my disgust verbally.

He didn't pay any attention to me but as we were getting ready to leave, he just happened to remember a couple of stories about deer that had been killed by men who used nothing but shotguns. Each big buck had collapsed in a heap when they were shot and never moved an inch—I didn't buy it. I bitched and bellyached and I felt sorry for myself in large numbers. When I started out with the rest of the crew I was positive that I was the most abused buck hunter in Bayfield County.

My Uncle Phil, Dad's youngest brother, had used the shotgun before he had a rifle and he had dropped it one day. Snow had lodged in the barrel and when he shot, the force of the charge expanded it so there was a bump or ridge about six inches from the muzzle. This never altered its accuracy but many people made comments about it and this added to my displeasure. It had been fine when I was a kid but now I was 14 and grown up!

When we left camp that morning it started to snow. The weather was quite mild and so it was thick, heavy, and wet. As we tramped through the woods it increased and when we finally spread out to make the drive, it was very disagreeable. Every bush spewed snow as we walked through the woods and each time

*A spectacular buck in a Missouri field. (Photo © Denver Bryan)*

I stooped to get under a windfall or a heavily laden branch, it would go down the back of my exposed neck. It didn't take long before I knew that I was the most unfortunate soul in the world.

Here I was, a great buckhunter. I was wet, and the prospects of seeing anything were few because anyone knew that deer bed down when it is snowing that heavily. But worst of all was my disgraceful demotion to the bearer of a lowly shotgun which of course was useless in slaying a deer unless he was ten feet away.

When we arrived at Hessey's Landing the tracks were no longer discernible and the drive was given up. My dad took out his watch and said, "Well, I tell you boys, I think we'll work towards camp. If we spread out we can make a drive east of Peggy's shack and come through those jacks. Pete and I will line up on the old tote road and the rest of you spread out and work towards us. Wiggles, you take the farthest point because you know that territory, but be sure that you stay this side of the Delta road.

This father of mine was really a clever man. If he couldn't succeed by his stories, he had one more angle to inflate—the ego of a 14-year-old kid and I was honored by his trust for the first quarter of a mile.

When I reached the trail that I was to turn on, I waved at the last man and we started the drive. Now my spirits sank again as I faced the wet driving snow. I had one thought in mind—getting back to camp and tying into the boiled dinner that I knew was simmering on the kitchen stove. I thought to myself, "Hunting on a day like this is sure one helluva lot of foolishness. I hope it snows all day so Loche will have to go back and I can use the carbine tomorrow."

Sometimes a kid uses his head. I can't explain why I did but I suppose it was because I had heard so many stories about the unexpected happening when you are deer hunting so I reacted naturally.

They were coming at me head on. When I blinked my eyes and realized that I was seeing deer my first thought was, "Oh, hell, it's only a doe and if I shoot, I'll catch it because we have plenty of camp meat. Just then I sighted the second one and I crouched behind the scrub oak that was on my right side. Now I hoped that there was a buck trailing behind but there was another doe and a fawn and then with head up and tail a rollin', he was coming up the pike. I waited for him and when he was within 20 yards, I stood up and blasted. He went down hard but as the other four deer scattered in all directions, he got back on his feet. Before he had made two jumps, I let him have it again and he spilled.

I ran over to where he was lying and I really didn't know what to do. I had killed a deer and it was a nice big buck. When my dad and Loche came over the hill I was still running back and forth between the tree where I had leaned the shotgun and the dead deer. I had my jacket off, I was holding my gloves in my hand, my knife was still in the sheath, and on one of my trips between the gun and the deer, I noticed that I left the shotgun cocked. Of course, I wasn't nervous or excited—just dazed and incoherent.

When I became conscious of their presence I wasn't whooping, shouting, or jumping up and down. I don't think I really realized what had happened until my dad leaned his rifle against a tree, took off his glove, extended his hand, grinned and said, "Congratulations, boy, that was damn fine shooting. I told you it could be done."

I shook his hand and his steel-like grip as well as his smile and the twinkle of his eye made me know that he was proud of me and I was truly ashamed of myself for the way I had acted.

After the deer was cleaned out, Dad and I had gone back to the trail that I was on when I had first sighted the deer and he had me reconstruct the event as it happened. He congratulated me a second time for realizing that there was usually a buck trailing the does. He wanted the facts straight so that he could file them in his mind for future reference. There might be another kid in camp some day who also balked at using a shotgun.

Many years later Charlie Willoughby, who was another great hunter at our camp for quite a few years, told me my dad's version of the story step by step. I hadn't realized how aware Dad was of my feelings of disgust, rebellion, and surliness on that day but when he told the story he must have given that angle quite a buildup because when Charlie told it to me, he didn't spare the horses about how I had acted and I was embarrassed until he hit the climax of the story.

*A magnificent buck with a towering rack. (Photo © T. Urban)*

Among the many fine skills my father had, one of them was mindreading!

At the dinner table there were quite a few stories told about other similar incidents and naturally my pride swelled. I was extremely proud when my Uncle Pete congratulated me as if I were a man.

The following Monday I was again promoted. Loche had to go back to school and so the carbine was mine to use again. Even though I had had success with the shotgun, I was overjoyed to again become a rifle hunter.

The morning drives were uneventful. We had seen deer but no one had any shooting at bucks. That afternoon when we had finished the first drive Dad mapped out the next one but he did not include me. After he had given the last man his assignment he said, "Now, Wiggles, I'm going to send you on a little trip by yourself. You follow this grade until you come to a big stand of hardwoods. Turn right on the far side and keep the sun on your right cheek. When you walk about a half of a mile, you will see that clump of jacks where you shot the buck. Make a check and see if everything is all right and then you can circle and come back home. By that time it should be quitting time so be sure that you don't miss the grade that leads to Hessey's Landing."

I followed his directions and found the buck without any trouble. We had covered him with brush as there was now the danger of having deer stolen. It had snowed more after we had cached him, so I bypassed the immediate area in case someone followed my tracks, and I headed for the grade.

There had not been too much snow that fall and so the walking was good. When I arrived at the grade that would take me back to camp I stopped and sat down on a windfall. I was quite proud of myself and as I sat there looking over the country I began to construct in my mind the story of my conquest. It had to be told in a nonchalant manner as if there was nothing unusual about shooting an eight-point buck and as I looked at the carbine and admired it, I decided that I would not even mention the weapon that I had used.

The sun had started to go down and after ten minutes of sitting I was getting chilly, so I decided

*A young whitetail buck limberly skips across a shallow lake in Maine. (Photo © Thomas D. Mangelsen/Images of Nature)*

that I had better start for home. After all, it was just as easy to dream while you were walking and after you have shot your buck, what else is new?

As I stood up and flexed my shoulders I looked across the large open area to my left. I could see the sun reflecting on the hillside about a half of a mile away and it glistened against the trees. Just then I saw him. He wasn't running, bounding, or leaping across the snow—he was lumbering towards me as if he had come a long ways and he was being pushed. I was fascinated as I observed his approach and as he came closer I could see that he was indeed a very large buck and as he plodded through the snow, I knew that he was tired.

This time I hadn't bothered to get out of sight. The buck was coming toward me but when he was about a hundred yards from me he pointed his nose towards the wind and slowly veered away from me. I put my rifle up to get a shot at him when I figured he wouldn't get any closer but about that time he stopped behind a large scrub oak.

Now I didn't know what to do. I couldn't tell whether or not he had suddenly turned left and started up the hill or stopped. I ran back and forth on the trail trying to figure out what he had done and because I couldn't see him and I didn't know what else to do, I aimed directly at the center of the scrub oak and pulled the trigger.

Holy lightening old Nellie, he was there. As I ran down the grade a few yards I saw him trying to pull himself up the hill and I went after him as fast as I could. Halfway up the hill was as far as he could go and when I got there he was stretched out and breathing his last.

Now it was getting dark and again I was panic stricken. Here was a buck that was the granddaddy of them all. As I stood looking at him I realized that he was what was commonly called a swamp buck and he was big. His horns were flat, he was a fourteen-pointer, and in the dark he looked almost black. I grabbed his rack to pull him over and I could move only his head.

Once more I pulled off my jacket, leaned my rifle up against a tree, reached for my hunting knife, and then realizing how incompetent I was, I shouted, "Pa!"

For the first few times that I called he couldn't

hear me and then when he did, he presumed that I was lost so he replied, "I'm over here. Keep walking and I'll call again."

I took a deep breath and shouted with all of the force that I could muster, "Pa, I shot another one!"

I had the snow all tramped down around the buck by the time he arrived. It seemed as if it took an awful long time for him to get there and my imagination ran wild with thoughts of his not being able to find me.

When he arrived and saw the buck he leaned his rifle against a tree, took off his jacket, dropped to his knees to examine the rack and said, "Well you sure as hell have a lot of fun, don't you?"

He didn't waste any time asking questions or congratulating me about this kill as it was getting dark fast, but when we had to make two attempts to get him on his back so that we could clean him out he warmed my heart by saying, "By the sweet smilin' Johanna boy, you sure pick 'em big. This one's the size of a young horse."

I had never heard that comparison before so I immediately filed it away to use when I would return to school and tell the kids about my prowess as a deer hunter.

My father never believed in starting a man too far up the ladder when he was teaching him the tricks of a new trade so on this cold November evening, I started my apprenticeship at field dressing deer at the bottom and I mean literally. When we had the buck turned over, I was crouched on my knees in back of him and I was holding a hind leg in each hand. He was spread-eagled and I was waiting for Dad to cut him open when he said, "Will that knife of yours cut anything?"

I was a little perturbed to think that he would have his doubts as I had spent hours sharpening it so I replied, "Uncle Pete said it was so sharp he could shave with it."

I handed it to him, he ran his thumb along the edge and said, "All right my boy, as long as you're so handy, you can rim him out."

My mouth dropped open, I stared at him and said, "Holy Gosh Pa, I don't want to do that dirty job."

"There's nothin' to it," he said, "just be careful and cut around the outside ridge. Go in the full

*A doe with its two fawns along the edge of a lily pad–covered pond. (Photo © Gregory M. Nelson)*

length of the blade and the whole shebang will come out as easy as pullin' off your sox."

He handed me his pocket knife that he had already opened. I had always admired that knife and I had seen him use it for many things on many occasions. The first thoughts that came to my mind were the apples that he had peeled for me and the number of times that I had watched him scrape the thin skin from the new potatoes freshly dug from the garden.

Admittedly, the knife was suited for this job as well. It had a long narrow blade, it was as sharp as a razor, and it had been honed to a needle point. I gulped a few times to keep my stomach from turning over, made a couple of bad cuts and then when I finally made up my mind that as detestable as it was, I had to use my left hand, I completed the job.

My biggest mistake was doing it too well because for the next two years that was always my job when I was with Dad.

It was always the same. Sometimes the deer would be shot before we had finished a drive and as the other drivers would come to look him over Dad would say, "That sure is a fine buck. Now you fellows spread out again and finish the drive and the boy and I will clean him out." Then again, it could happen this way—the buck would be killed at the end of a drive and once more the men would gather around to admire him and hear the story. As it didn't make sense for everyone to stand around while there was still daylight and there were deer to be hunted, Dad would give the orders for the next drive, "Now you fellows follow this grade to the Delta road and then spread out. Work toward Canthook Lake and the boy and I will take care of this fellow. Take your time walking down there so we can get over there and station ourselves. We'll be on the big ridge above that stand of hardwood."

As the men would start down the grade he would pull off his jacket, take his knife from his back pocket and handing it to me would say, "Well, we better get started. You can rim him out!"

When I was a senior in high school, I was finally promoted.

Getting back to the swamp buck—after we had cleaned him out Dad said, "Well as long as you killed him, you can carry the heart and liver."

In the past years I have come across many places in the woods where a deer had been field dressed and invariably the heart and liver would be left. We always brought them back to camp because this was a meal that was always enjoyed by the old time hunters. Fried with bacon and onions, it was fit for a king.

Every hunter in our camp always cut a forked branch to carry them on except my dad. He would wrap them in his large red bandanna, knot the ends together and then tie it to the belt loops on the back of his trousers with the inevitable piece of string that he always carried so that he would have both hands free, "Just in case there was a little action."

It was while I was searching for a suitable branch that I received the second revolting shock of the day. I found out in later years that it was a common procedure among the old timers but at the moment besides being shocked out of my wits, I was horrified and ashamed for him.

He had turned so that he had his back to me and by his stance, I presumed that he was relieving himself. What I didn't know and what made me almost petrified with horror was to realize that he was also rinsing his hands. I stared and then screamed, "Pa, for gosh sakes what are you doing?"

He looked my way and said, "I'm getting the blood off my hands. What in hell did you think I was doing?"

I gulped and said, "But for gosh sakes, not like that."

Again he calmly replied, "Well, you don't think I'd be damn fool enough to put my hands in that cold snow do you?"

I stuttered and stammered but said no more.

The moon was high when we reached the grade that would lead us to camp. Again we had broken and cut branches to cover the buck and then we kicked snow on top of them so that it looked like any other of the many hummocks on the hillside.

I really enjoyed our hike back. It was cold but the air was so clear and still that the only sound was the snow crunching under our boots as we followed the trail. The country was not grown up in those days and in the moonlight the clumps of jackpines and the many stumps were easily distinguishable against the snow. Every once in awhile Dad would stop and call my attention to a spot where Uncle Miller had

*Nearly silhouetted by the morning sunlight, a large buck with his tall rack of antlers watches warily for danger. (Photo © T. Urban)*

killed a buck, or where Harry Hall had shot two does while he sat on a stump relacing his boot, or he would point out the old tote road that stretched like a white ribbon among the trees. I was hungry, tired, and anxious to get back to camp so that I could again bask in the limelight, but our conversation made me feel good. To me it seemed as if for the first time, he was talking to me on a man-to-man basis instead as a father to his youngest son.

The lamps glowing in the windows of the cabin certainly looked inviting as we turned off the Pole road and started down the South trail and I could hardly wait to make my grand entrance.

Even though I felt that I was growing up fast I didn't attempt to give any detailed account of my success. I admitted that my shot had been a lucky one as I didn't know the buck was behind the scrub oak but my dad told the story.

When we hauled in the deer the next day, they had all agreed that my swamp buck was the biggest one that they had seen for some time and I glowed with pride as the men admired him.

I have a picture of that buck and a partial picture of myself standing beside him. When my sister Lylith snapped the shutter, it was the last exposure on the roll. I don't know whether she was aware of the fact that she cut me off at the shoulders but at least it is a nice picture of the buck.

A few weeks later George Buchanan of Ashland, a friend of the family, came over to see Dad on business. When he saw the size of the horns he wanted the head so that he could have it mounted. He offered me $3.00 for it and I hesitated—about two seconds.

I often wondered about George's story when someone would come in his office and see that mounted head on the wall. It must have been a wonderful conversation piece and I would bet dollars to doughnuts that it broke the ice for his sales pitch to a prospective customer more than once. I used to hope that he would at least start his story by saying, "One fall when I was hunting at Hakon Lund's camp south of Iron River . . ."

Left: *After eating its fill, a Florida buck beds down in a secure area away from predators. (Photo © Chica Stracener)*
Overleaf: *Whitetails search for food as the sun begins to rise above the morning fog in Michigan. (Photo © Bruce Montagne)*

# THE HUNTING LESSON

## by Patrick F. McManus

Patrick F. McManus needs little introduction. He is America's outdoor humorist without peer, author of a large body of stories over the past few decades. He writes in a jocular, over-the-top style that blends the irony of Mark Twain with the bravado of Ernest Hemingway to create tall tales that are all McManus.

With more than ten books in print, including *They Shoot Canoes, Don't They?*, *A Fine and Pleasant Misery,* and *The Night The Bear Ate Goombaw,* McManus's stories detail his sporting misadventures, from whitetail hunting to fishing with worms. This story from *The Grasshopper Trap* describes just such a failure—a hunting lesson that backfires.

Over the years it has been my distinct honor and pleasure to introduce numerous persons to the sport of hunting. It is odd, however, that a man can have a thousand successes and one failure, and it will be the failure that sticks in his mind like a porky quill in a hound's nose. Thus it is with my single failure, one Sidney Sample. Even now, five years later, I torment myself with the question of where I went wrong. How did I slip with Sample?

The affair started off innocently enough. One fall day, with none of my regular hunting partners available for the following weekend, I strolled next door to Sidney's house to invite him to go deer hunting with me. I found him digging up bulbs in the garden, and greeted him informally, namely by sneaking up behind him and dumping a basket of moldering leaves over his head. Not one to enjoy a good joke on himself, Sidney growled malevolently and thrust blindly at me with the garden trowel.

"Sidney," I said, holding him at bay with a rake handle, "I am about to give you the opportunity of a lifetime. How would you like to go deer hunting with me?"

"Not much," he replied, fingering leaf mold from his ears. "In fact, my desire to go hunting with you is so slight as to escape detection by modern science!"

"Don't like hunting, huh?" I said. "Well, many people who have never been exposed to the sport feel that way about it. Listen, I can teach you all about hunting. One weekend out with me, and you'll come back loving it."

"No," Sidney snarled.

"If nothing else, you'll enjoy getting out in the crisp mountain air. It will invigorate you."

"No! No! *NO!*"

"Sid, I just know you'll enjoy the camaraderie of the hunting camp, the thrill of the pursuit, the . . ."

*A whitetail buck leaps over a fallen tree. (Photo © Jerry and Barbara Jividen/Images Unique)*

"No, I tell you, no! Go *home!*"

". . . the free meat and . . ."

"Free meat?"

"Sure. Just think of packing away all those free venison steaks and chops and roasts in the freezer."

"Free meat. Venison's good, too. I tasted it once. Yeah, I wouldn't mind getting a bunch of free meat. Then, too, as you say, there's the hunting-camp camaraderie, the crisp mountain air, and the thrill of pursuit. But I'm willing to put up with all that stuff if I can get some free meat."

I would have patted him on the shoulder, but I didn't want to get my hands all dirty with leaf mold. "I can see right now you have the makings of a true sportsman," I told him.

"So how do I get this free deer?" Sidney asked.

"Well, you just go out with me and get it. Of course, there are a few odds and ends you'll need to pick up down at Duffy's Sporting Goods."

"Like what?"

"Oh, let's see. You'll need a rifle, of course. Outfitted with scope and sling. A couple boxes of shells. Seems to me there's something else. A knife! You'll need a good hunting knife. And a whetstone. I nearly forgot the whetstone. That should be about it. You have a good pair of insulated boots, don't you? No? Oh, wool pants, you'll need wool pants and some good wool socks and a wool shirt and a down parka and some thermal underwear and an orange hunting vest and a red cap. Heck, that should do it. Good, you're making a list. Did I say gloves? Get some gloves. Oh, binoculars! And a first-aid kit. And a survival kit, with a daypack to carry it in. Rope, you'll need a length of rope for dragging your free deer out of the mountains with. We could use my tent, of course, but it has a rip in the roof on the guest's side. You might want to buy a tent. A subzero sleeping bag, did I mention that? You'll probably want an insulated sleeping pad, too. Down booties are awfully nice to slip into when you take off your hunting boots, but they're optional. Then there's the grub, and that's it. Did I mention the hunting license and deer tag?"

"Hmmmm," Sidney said, studying his list. "Just how big are these free deer, anyway?"

*Veiled by the morning mist, a buck hunts for food. (Photo © Len Rue, Jr.)*

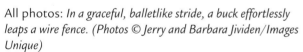

All photos: *In a graceful, balletlike stride, a buck effortlessly leaps a wire fence. (Photos © Jerry and Barbara Jividen/Images Unique)*

"Big!" I said. "Real big!"

"Geez," he said, "I don't know how I can afford to buy all the stuff on this list."

"Take some advice from an old experienced hunter—mortgage the house."

After Sidney purchased his outfit, I took him out to the gun-club range and we sighted in his rifle. He grouped his last five shots right in the center of the bull's-eye. Then I showed him my technique of scattering shots randomly around the target because, as I explained, you never know which way the deer might jump just as you pull the trigger.

"How long before I learn to do that?" Sidney asked.

"Years," I said. "It's not something you master overnight."

The day before the hunt, Retch Sweeney called up and said he would be able to go hunting after all.

"How come he's going?" Sidney snapped when I told him the news. They are not exactly bosom buddies.

"He's between jobs," I said.

"I didn't know he ever worked," Sidney growled. "When did he get laid off?"

"Nineteen fifty-seven."

I explained to Sidney the absolute necessity of being ready when Retch and I came to pick him up the next morning. "We'll arrive at your house at two sharp. Got that? *Two sharp!*"

"Right," he said.

"Don't bother about breakfast. We can grab a quick bite at Greasy Gert's Gas 'n' Grub just before we turn off the highway and head up to our hunting area. Now remember, *two sharp!*"

We picked Sidney up the next morning at exactly 5:35. He was furious. Naturally, Retch and I were puzzled. Then it occurred to me that since this was Sidney's first hunt, he didn't realize that when hunters say "two sharp," they mean "sometime around five."

"Stop whimpering and toss your gear in back," Retch said. "You better not have forgot nothin' either, because we're not turnin' around and comin' back for it! Now put your rifle in the rack next to mine."

"What do you mean, next to yours?"

"That ol' .30-06 right there . . . Say, I wonder if you fellas would mind swingin' by my house again.

Just take a few minutes."

After Retch had picked up his rifle and I had returned to my house for my sleeping bag and then we had gone back to Retch's for his shells, it was almost six-thirty by the time we got out to the highway.

"Aren't we going to be awfully late with all these delays?" Sidney asked. "What time will we start hunting?"

Retch and I looked at each other and laughed. "Why, man, we're already hunting!" Retch said. "This is it. This is what hunting's all about."

We drove along for an hour, as Retch and I entertained Sidney with detailed accounts of other hunting trips. "It was a tough shot, looked impossible to me at first," Retch was saying. "That six-point buck was going away from me at an angle and . . ."

I held up my hand for silence. "Okay, now we got to get serious. We're coming to the most dangerous part of the trip. We get through this ordeal and we should be okay. You guys watch yourselves. If you start to feel faint or queasy, Sid, let me know right away."

"Cripes!" Sidney said nervously. "What do we have to do, drive up a sheer cliff or something?"

"Worse," I said. "We're going to eat breakfast at Greasy Gert's."

Dawn had long since cracked and spilled over the mountains by the time we arrived at our hunting spot. Retch looked out the window and groaned.

"What are you groaning for?" I asked. "I'm the one that had Gerty's chili-pepper omelette."

It's not that," Retch said. "I see fresh tracks in the snow all over the place. If we'd been here an hour earlier, we'd have nailed us some deer."

"Listen," I said. "Did we come out to nail deer or to go hunting today? If we're hunting, we have to get up two hours late, forget a bunch of stuff we have to go back for, and then stop for breakfast at Gerty's. You know how it's done."

"Yeah, sorry, I forgot for a second when I saw the tracks," Retch said. "I got carried away. Who cares about nailing deer right off!"

"I do!" Sidney yelped. "I just bought twenty-five hundred dollars worth of hunting stuff, and I want to get my free deer!"

It was clear that Sidney had a lot to learn about hunting, so I lost no time in starting on his first lesson. I put him on a stand and told him that Retch

and I would sweep around the far side of the ridge and drive some deer past him. "We'll be back in an hour," I told him. "Don't move!"

Retch and I returned three hours later and found Sidney still on the stand. He was frosted over and stiff as an icicle. We leaned him against a tree until we got a fire going to thaw him out.

"How come you didn't move around?" I asked him.

"Y-you t-told me to stay on the st-stand. You said y-you would be b-back in an hour, and for me not to m-move."

"I'm sorry, I should have explained," I said. "When a hunter says he'll be back in an hour, that means not less than three hours. Furthermore, nobody ever stays on a stand as he's told to. As soon as the other hunters are out of sight, he beats it off to some other place where he's sure there's a deer but there never is. That's standard procedure. I guess I should have mentioned it to you."

"Yeah," Retch said. "Anyway, next time you'll know. It takes a while to catch on to deer hunting. Well, we might as well make camp. We ain't gonna get no deer today."

"Oh, I got one!" Sidney said. "See, he's lying over there behind that log. He was too big for me to move by myself. Right after you fellows left, he came tearing along the trail there, and I shot him."

"Oh-oh!" I said. "Better go have a look, Retch."

Retch walked over to the deer, looked down, shook his head, and walked back.

"We're in for it now," he told me.

"How bad is it?" I asked.

"Six points."

"Cripes!" I said.

"Did I do it wrong?" Sidney asked.

"We'll have to wait and see," I said.

Sidney thought for a moment, then smiled. "Gee, wouldn't it be funny if I was the only one to get a deer and it was my first trip and all, and you guys were teaching me how to hunt. Not that I would ever mention it to the guys down at Kelly's Bar & Grill, but . . . Is six points good? Say, let me tell you how I got him. It was a tough shot, looked impossible to me at first. The six-point buck was going away from me at an angle, and . . ."

"It's going to be even worse than I first thought," Retch said.

"Yeah," I said. "Ol' Sidney learns fast. Well, you can't win 'em all."

*A majestic whitetail buck in South Texas. (Photo © Steve Bentsen)*

# Chapter 2

# THE GLORY AND THE MISERY OF THE HUNT

*For many years I have been telling the boys of the big bucks I have killed, the wild turkeys I have slain, the grouse and ringnecks and quail that have been blasted by my blunderbuss. And, strange to say, I have been telling the truth. But my soul feels sinful; dark secrets lurk in it. The reason for this apprehension is that I have been confining my tales to what I did, keeping artfully suppressed what I did not do.*
—Archibald Rutledge, "Great Misses I Have Made," 1939

# THE TEST OF
# A DEER STAND

## by Tom Anderson

Tom Anderson is well versed in the miseries of deer hunting. A deer and bird hunter as well as a fisherman, he has suffered for his art, whether it be in an ice-fishing house or on a frigid Minnesota deer stand in late fall.

Anderson has worked for more than a decade as a teacher and naturalist for the Lee and Rose Warner Nature Center in Marine-on-St. Croix, Minnesota, which is operated by the Science Museum of Minnesota. He also writes an award-winning column for the *Chisago County Press*. He collected his columns into a book, *Learning Nature by a Country Road*, from which this essay on the peculiar adversity of the deer stand was chosen.

Under the illumination of the yard light, I checked the thermometer on the woodshed. It read a couple of degrees below zero. Fifteen minutes later, I was eight feet off the ground in a wind-split red oak, settling down to wait for a deer. All was quiet except for one great horned owl just to the north of me and another to the south. Their duet finished as dawn's ashen colors paled toward the break of a new day.

I sat feeling comfortable, warmed by the brisk hike I had taken across a couple of bean fields and a piece of woods before climbing into the tree. However, the glow of warmth was short-lived, and a slight shiver rippled across my shoulders. I knew it would take tremendous patience and fortitude to remain motionless in my perch on this morning, so I tried to combat the chill by concentrating on warm thoughts.

My mind traveled back a mere thirty minutes to when I sleepily crawled out from under a warm down comforter and slowly dressed while standing on the floor grate, which spewed out a rising flow of hot air. My warm thoughts were shattered when I heard the ominous noises of new lake ice, nearly a quarter-mile away, booming and groaning. The ice-sounds clearly remind me that the hot floor grate was a quarter-mile in the opposite direction.

Daylight was slow in coming, and the spasms of shudders became more frequent. I am convinced that there is nothing colder than waiting in a November or December deer stand for the passing of a buck.

Pages 48–49: *Its breath condensing in the cool dawn air, a Montana whitetail buck stands atop a hillock. (Photo © D. Robert Franz)*

Page 49, inset: *The glory of hunting, twelve times over. Following a three-day hunt in northern Wisconsin in the 1880s, these hunters are ready for some well-deserved rest. (Photo by S. A. Johnson, courtesy Minnesota Historical Society)*

Facing page: *A Michigan buck amid a stand of heavily rubbed young trees, following a winter storm. (Photo © Gregory M. Nelson)*

Some might argue that ice fishing is a colder endeavor, and sometimes it is, but at least when I ice fish, I don't have to keep still. The law says I can fish from two holes, and if I put them a little ways from each other, I can trot from hole to hole. I can walk circles, do jumping jacks, or bore more holes with my ice auger.

Put simply, when the muscles work, the by-product is the creation of heat. But on a deer stand, much of my success as a deer hunter will stem from my ability to sit motionless.

I could see the makings of a glow in the east, and I wished that the glowing orb of swirling gases that we call our sun, some ninety-three million miles away, would hurry and send some of its heat my way. It has been estimated that the sun's surface is a toasty six thousand degrees Celsius. I only wished for a fraction of that to wash over my frigid form.

Before the sun was even up, my hands, hidden in my chopper mitts, were balled in fists to slow the heat loss from my fingers. Likewise, my toes were numbing, so I concentrated on wriggling them—first the left foot, then the right one, and so on. I played host to dreams of performing a hard driving tap dance shoed in Sorel boots—something that Fred Astaire or Gene Kelly have never done.

I tried convincing myself that it really wasn't that cold by entertaining thoughts of boyhood days scampering as fast as I could across a blacktopped street that had absorbed July's sizzling heat. The summery dream was disturbed by the sharp, riflelike report of a popping tree. All around me, the dawn's stillness was occasionally shattered by trees as their sapwood froze, expanded, and cracked.

I've never considered a deer stand to be known for its comfort—it's the view that counts. I want to see what is going on and yet remain relatively hidden up in the limbs off the ground. Usually, I find a climbable tree and make my way carefully up into the branches. Climbing or shinnying up a tree is not easy when one resembles a fat, orange sausage.

My deer stands are usually just a perch in the limbs of a tree. On a rare occasion I may nail up a step or two or a single board to stand on. The simpler the better. In fact, if I get too comfortable, I run

*Stretched out while running, the whitetail's body is sleek and built for speed. (Photo © Jeanne Drake, Las Vegas, NV)*

the risk of dozing off and dreaming of deer instead of hunting them. But on the other hand, if I can get comfortable I can stay in my deer stand longer and better maintain my vigil over this corner of the woods. If I am a little uncomfortable, sleep is less likely, and I can remain more alert, though my stay among the branches might not be so long.

A neighbor has a crudely assembled platform complete with an old sofa to luxuriate in. I'm afraid I couldn't stay awake for very long in such a stand.

Tales used to float around about the local cobbler who, with others in his gang, hunted the north-woods near Superior's shores for a span of twenty years. He believed in being comfortable if he was going to subject himself to November's unpredictable weather. His deer stand had four walls, complete with a sliding glass window and a roof. Warmed by a gas heater, listening to a portable radio, he could just as well have been back in his shoe shop. You might think he could spend a day or two in such a stand, but he was by nature a restless man. Others in his party claimed that on opening morning, they could hear the cobbler hammering on his stand back in the woods as he revamped or added on to his cabin in the trees.

I also heard that he never shot a deer—but he was comfortable, while others in his party shivered and got him his venison.

There is a local farmer who hunted his woods in comfort. He liked to stay closer to the ground, so he would annually pull his ice fishing house out in the woods, fire up the stove and sit peering through the window.

Even with the awakening of the sun, I was still cold. It was apparent that I could not retain my heat, so I tried producing some. From under my seven layers of clothes that covered my upper body and the three that protected my lower trunk, I tensed my muscles as if I were pushing a car out of a snow-filled ditch. Then I relaxed briefly before repeating the isometrics.

Every year it seems that I must be painfully reminded of the suffering involved if I'm to take to a November deer stand. It's the price you have to pay. When I got to work the next day and was reliving the cold morning of the day before with a co-worker, she replied, "It must be like having a baby, you forget from one baby to the next just how awful the experience can be."

Finally, I had all I could take. Any more suffering would be masochistic. It seemed an effort to make my legs work as I climbed down. Since I had not seen a single deer, the cold ordeal had seemingly been worse than it was.

I figure if I'm not going to see any deer I might just as well go talk to the cobbler and see if he would share his deer stand blueprints with me.

Facing page: *A magnificent buck surveys its domain. (Photo © D. Robert Franz)*
Overleaf: *Whitetail country: A creek winds its way through a Montana valley etched in frost. (Photo © Jerry and Barbara Jividen/ Images Unique)*

# YOU'VE GOT TO SUFFER!

## by Gordon MacQuarrie

Gordon MacQuarrie remained true to Wisconsin all of his years. Born in Superior, in the northwestern part of the state, he hunted duck and deer in the marshes, fields, and forests of dairyland throughout his life. He was a writer and editor for the *Superior Evening Telegram* before moving on to the *Milwaukee Journal*, where he worked for over two decades as the outdoor editor.

Of all his writings, his series of columns from the 1940s through the 1950s chronicling the fictitious Old Duck Hunters' Association earned him the most loyal following. Led by their Old Man—the President of the Association—in his famous brown mackinaw, the Old Duck Hunters stalked duck and deer through thick and thin, imparting their philosophy of living along the way. MacQuarrie's columns were collected into a series of three books, *Stories of the Old Duck Hunters & Other Drivel*, *More Stories of the Old Duck Hunters*, and *Last Stories of the Old Duck Hunters*. This tale of deer hunting during the coldest season opener on record is classic MacQuarrie.

The President of the Old Duck Hunters' Association, Inc., was waiting for me; so I had to get in there, even if the snow was a foot deep on the level and heavily drifted. I lay on my back in city clothes to jack up the rear wheels for tire chains, wishing that the guy who had designed those petticoat fenders was properly punished for his sins against a humanity which at some time or other simply must use auto chains.

The chains, momentum and good luck took me into a solid three-foot drift. Well, I got halfway through it. A half hour of shoveling ensued, and then I turned off the back road on the narrow, twisting by-road.

It was a shambles of drooping pine trees. Jack-pines thirty feet tall and up to five inches thick were arched over the road, weighted down under tons of damp snow. A few clips with the pocket-ax which I always carried in the car snapped them; then it was necessary to shake the clinging snow from them and drag them off the road.

There would be no deer hunting the next day—I was sure of that. Getting about in that snow would be impossible. But I had said I would get in there. The Old Man was waiting. It is amazing what a man will do to keep a date with the President of the Old Duck Hunters.

*A whitetail buck stands out from the snow-covered landscape. (Photo © Doug Locke)*

I was six hours behind schedule when I stopped the car beside Mister President's snow-shrouded car. I was sweating and unsteady afoot. There had been almost a whole day of nerve-racking driving in the storm before the final climactic effort to get over that last half mile. I grabbed pack-sack and rifle and wallowed to the door of the place.

The Old Man was asleep, with his feet stretched toward the fireplace. I moved quietly. I put new wood on his fire, broke out duffle and had the teakettle going in the kitchen before he awoke. He called from the big room, "That you, Tom?"

"Yep," I answered, sounding as much like Tom as I could.

"When did you get here?"

"Minute ago."

Tom is a neighbor who is likely to appear at the abode of the Old Duck Hunters almost any time. The Old Man continued, still unsuspecting:

"Where do you suppose that whelp of a boy is? Said he'd be here for supper, and it's midnight."

I heard him yawn and heard him wind his watch. Then he said: "Dammit, Tom, I'm worried. He might try to make it here in this storm, and he doesn't know the first thing about driving a car in snow."

"And never will. Don't worry about him. He'll hole up in some luxurious hotel down the line and wait for the snow-plows."

That speech was too long. The Old Man's feet hit the floor, and he stamped to the kitchen, all sympathy vanished.

"You pup of a boy!" he snorted. "You lame-brained rooster!" He carried on over a snack of tea and toast. "Cars stuck all over the country. This is the worst storm ever hit this country before a deer season opening."

I looked around. He had brought in enough wood to last for several days. I said, "We'll just hole up, as long as we can't hunt."

"Not hunt!"

He had it all figured out. He'd looked over the near-by thoroughfare country in the storm and had found deer working down into it, out of the more open jack-pine on higher ground.

"We'll hunt, all right!"

That was the last thing I heard before dropping off to sleep. I think I did not change my position

once, and slept until noon, right around the clock.

"I'm saving you," he explained. "Had to get you in shape. You're going to make one little drive to me."

"I'm not mooching in this snow."

The Old Man pointed to the wall at the end of the room. "See those snowshoes? All you've done to them the last two years is varnish 'em. Today you're going to wear off some varnish."

It was bitter cold, near zero, after the snow had ceased and the clouds passed. All right, if the Old Man was going to sit on a stump in that weather, he was going to put on some clothing. I persuaded him, over his objections, to pile on plenty of underwear, a wool sweatshirt and a heavy outer shirt. He bulged rather ridiculously, I had to admit, with all that clothing, but for good measure I made him carry along my huge, ungainly but wonderfully warm sheep-lined aviation boots.

He hated the clothes that bore him down. I knew what he wanted to wear—just his regular duck or deer-season gear, which is not too much, topped off with the old brown mackinaw. He vowed that the only way a man could wait out a deer was to do a little personal freezing.

I had to laugh when he started out. He was so swaddled in clothes that he could hardly turn his neck above the shawl collar of the ancient mackinaw. But I did not laugh, for I was afraid he'd go back into the house and shed some of the garments, and in that searching cold I could not see him suffering while I took what is really the easier course, moving and so keeping warm.

South of us lay the Norway pine hill facing the thoroughfare, or river, between two lakes. Mister President had it all figured out. He would take an old stand at the top of the Norway hill. I would circle to the south and west of him, then drive up through the thick cover lying at the edge of the thoroughfare. If anything with horns came through, he would have shooting as it hit the open Norway grove.

Northwest Wisconsin, in twenty years, never saw a storm like that one at that season. Nor did it, in that time, see cold like that so early, combined with deep snow. The freak storm kept hundreds out of the bush. It was the first day of the four-day buck season. We had the country practically to ourselves. Most of the army of hunters was waiting for the snow

*A whitetail buck stands guard over a fawn. (Photo © Len Rue, Jr.)*

*A whitetail buck stands tall, silhouetted on the horizon. (Photo © Michael H. Francis)*

to settle or thaw. And a four-day doe season was coming up in seven days.

Mister President's self-imposed assignment was to mush through the snow for about a mile, hard going without snowshoes, which he does not like. I left him plodding through the stuff toward his stand and began the great circle which would bring me below him.

At any rate, that snow was good for snowshoeing. It had the solid permanence of snow that has lain and settled and proposes to stay until spring—which it most certainly did.

It felt good to be on snowshoes again, carrying a rifle. I went through a long pulpwood slashing. All the tracks in that slashing confirmed what Mister President had said—that deer were moving into the denser cover, away from the open pinelands. Down there along the thoroughfare's edge they could find protection and browse, even some white cedar—champion of all winter deer browse.

The slashing was lovely. A bluejay yammered at me. Chickadees hung upside down on branches. Will someone tell me how these minute wisps of down maintain their high spirits in the face of any weather? A red squirrel in a jackpine cussed me roundly: "Bad enough for this storm to come so early without you moving in on my property!"

Snow-bent jacks lopped to the southwest, for the snow had come from the northeast, off Lake Superior. That storm gave the North a wonderful pruning. Old Lady Nature every so often throws one like that over her wild garden to nip off old branches, weed out the weak ones and compel the strong ones to prove it.

There was plenty of snow down my neck. Charlie Garvey, the forest ranger at Gordon, had warned me the evening before: "Stuff is down so much the rabbits can't get through." He knew, too, that the impact of this storm had pushed vast supplies of browse within reach of hungry deer. Incidentally, before winter was finished in the North, the sly dame did the same thing on two more occasions. So that deer got plenty to eat and the forests had a splendid pruning.

When I got to the thoroughfare where I was to turn back and drive north, I sat down a minute. At this place the thoroughfare drops three feet. There were wings overhead, belated bluebills and early golden-eyes hunting water in the frozen lake country.

The sun was varnishing the jack-pine tops as I began the drive. In the shadows the snow was turning lavender. Downy and hairy woodpeckers hid behind tree trunks as I went along. The snowshoes creaked. I followed the thoroughfare edge. There was ice out from shore forty yards at my right. At my left and ahead of me was thick cover.

There were many tracks, all old ones. Deer had certainly come down here out of the pinelands in the night. But where were they now? Then I saw a fresh track. You know how it is—that virgin white scar of a hoof in snow, so unlike the settled, stiffened track of twelve hours before.

The deer was moving ahead of me. Buck or doe? I do not know. Even in fresh mud I do not know, and I think that no one else can tell for certain. That track was big and brand-new. It was a mark left by a critter moving exactly the way the Old Duck Hunters wanted it to move—straight north toward the Old Man.

This deer was not plunging. It seemed to know my pace and kept just ahead of me. Likely it had heard me when I was a hundred yards away from it, had got up quietly and just sneaked away from me. You wonder at such times where the rascals get the wisdom to know that a man in snow cannot move rapidly. Deer can be very contemptuous of a man.

The wind was not a factor. There was a little drift from the northwest. Up in the open slashings it could be felt. Down along the thoroughfare bottoms, however, pipe smoke went straight up.

Sometimes this deer stayed on the beaten trails which had been worked in the night before. Sometimes it cut across lots through fresh snow. Contemptuous of me? Indeed, and then some.

I saw where, during the night of the storm, deer had come into the thoroughfare bottoms and nibbled on cedar. Even the little fellows could live off a storm like that. Everything was caved in, trees formed solid white wigwams, branches drooped—as inviting a deer cafeteria as you might wish to see.

Why hadn't this big one moved out of the bottoms with the others? Was it an old grandfather or a grandmother that chose the easy living of this place to getting out of there and seeing country? Once I thought I saw it a hundred yards ahead, but that turned out to be mere flipping of white snow from a branch released from pressure—not a flag.

My deer had passed the place where the snow slid off the tree, a full twenty yards to the west. A calculating beggar, that animal. Just so far ahead of me—no farther.

Well, if a buck, it was venison on the pole. It went dead on toward a rendezvous with a .30-30 carbine held by a very steady old gentleman in an old brown mackinaw.

That critter had me figured out so well that sometimes it even stopped to browse. It would pay for that—if it was what Mister President called "a rooster deer." Contempt of court, that's what it was! Just wait until that old goat moved out from the thick stuff and started ambling through those open Norways! The Old Man has killed a half dozen bucks from that stand. Most of them have dropped within an area not larger than a baseball diamond.

Good, I thought. Whatever it was, it was right on the beam going in. The darkness drew down. Purple worked up to the zenith from the eastern sky. I moved that deer along the way a farm collie brings home the cows. Finally I saw him.

He was across an opening, perhaps a hundred yards off. He was big and dim. No question now what he was. He was "he." His rack went up and back like branches on an old oak. I might have had one quick fling at him, but why chance it? The Old Man was waiting, and it was better to move that deer into the open Norway grove. Then, if the first one didn't clip him, there would be other chances.

I went along. I know that terrain as well as the buck knew it—almost as well as the Old Man knows it. Pretty soon, up ahead, there would be a shot. Just one shot, it ought to be. That would be the Old Man's 150 grains of lead and copper going to its destination. Then silence—the sort of quiet after one shot that means so much to a deer hunter.

It was working out perfectly. In my mind's eye I pictured the Old Man, alert on his hillside. I saw him scan the cover, saw the buck walk out and turn to listen along its back trail. I saw Mister President draw down on the buck, wait until the buck stood with cupped ears, raise the little rifle and squeeze it off. Yes, I even pictured him setting down the rifle and reaching for the big, bone-handled clasp-knife in his right hip pocket.

*Four whitetails lunge through a stream. (Photo © Jeanne Drake, Las Vegas, NV)*

It was as easy as falling off a log. Mister President's formula had been right. If the ground had been bare, that buck might have busted through the Norway grove with his foot to the floorboard.

I wondered if we should drag him the mile home. Or if we should borrow Hank's toboggan, or just commandeer his truck which has high wheels and is at home in deep snow. I decided that with the weather cold as it was we could dress him, hang him, cool him and have decent steaks by supper-time tomorrow.

Minutes passed. The Old Man would let him have it now. . . . Or now. . . . Now, then! The buck must be in the Norways at the foot of the hillside. Heavens above, he must be halfway up the hillside! I could see the big Norways ahead of me. The only sound was the creak of the snowshoes and the "kra-a-a-ak" of a raven.

I broke through the bottomland cover and faced the hillside. Over the hilltop in back of the old man I saw the buck the second time, slowly and contemptuously effacing himself from me.

I took one quick shot. It was just a shot at a skulking shadow, and I knew as I pulled the trigger in the instant I had for shooting that I was over him a good two or three feet.

At the shot Mister President waved to me from his stand. I trudged up the hill to him. He looked guilty.

"You git 'im?"

"Mister President, do not speak to me ever again."

He made a clean breast of it, then and there. "All right, I fell asleep. Your shot woke me."

It was plain as sin what had happened. Mister President had brushed the snow off a fallen Norway and sat there a while. He had lit a fire. He had banked browse against that two-foot-thick down log so that he could stretch out. Then—oh, my brethren!—he had fallen asleep. "Dammit, I had too many clothes on," he said.

And then I just had to laugh. He wasn't the Mister President of other deer drives, chilled and lean and ready, with a drop on the end of his nose. He was swathed and cluttered sleep-producing items—those huge aviator's boots, which are with clothes, and over his swampers he had drawn the final, comparable to separate steam-heating systems.

We went home, boiled the kettle, and ate pork chops and boiled potatoes. We drank quarts of tea. At bedtime the Old Man announced: "If anyone tries to tell me what to wear tomorrow, I will resign the presidency of the Old Duck Hunters. I must have dozed there for two hours."

The next day we did it again. The weather had moderated. He went to the same stand. I made the long swing south and west on the snowshoes and drove up through the thoroughfare bottoms. Making the drive, I knew that now the Old Man was standing there by his down log, in his thin swampers, I knew that sometimes he shivered, and sometimes he whapped his arms across his breast to get circulation going. I knew that he'd move up and down on his feet and wriggle his toes, and that he was standing there with his earlaps up, so that he could hear better.

The drive was easy. There were more deer in the bottoms along the thoroughfare. Driving up through and watching the tracks ahead of me, I felt that I was pushing a whole herd into that Norway grove. One of them might be Old Horny, might be the same old fellow who beat the Old Duck Hunters yesterday, hands down.

Pow! He had shot just once. I came into the grove at the foot of the hillside, and Mister President called down to me: "He's lying over to your left. Four hens came out, and the rooster after them."

I do not know whether it was the same buck. I think it was another. The one of the day before seemed a larger animal. There he was, a good tenpointer. I called up the hill: "Bring your knife down here, and I'll dress him out."

He came sliding down the hill in the snow. "I'll dress him out myself. Maybe I can get warmed up that way."

Mister President was certainly a sight. His nose was red and his lips were blue. He was hunched and shivering beneath the old brown mackinaw. The wait in the cold had been a long one, but worth it. He went to work, and I went off to fetch Hank with his truck. When we got back, the Old Man had finished the job—had even dragged the buck up his hillside and out to the road to meet the truck.

"Well, you sure got warmed up," I said.

"I did," he agreed. "But you got to suffer first."

*Backlit by the summer sun, the velvet on this buck's antlers seems to glow. (Photo © D. Robert Franz)*

# Chapter 3

# BUCK FEVER

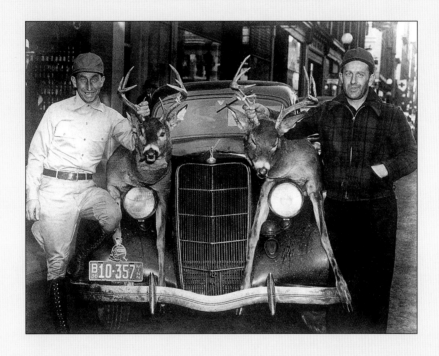

*As a chronic sufferer from buck fever, quail fever, and ram fever, I speak from deep and bitter experience. . . . Curiously, I feel no shame at my weakness, for it is my belief that the keener the hunter, the more he respects and admires the game he seeks, the more likely he is at any time to succumb to an attack of buck fever.*

*—Jack O'Connor, "I Get Buck Fever . . . and I Like It," 1936*

# MISTER HOWARD
# WAS A REAL GENT

## by Robert Ruark

The late Robert Ruark is perhaps the best-loved writer of outdoor literature. Like Ernest Hemingway, Ruark was a journalist as well as a best-selling author; his novels include *Poor No More, Uhuru,* and *Something of Value.* But many remember him best for his well-crafted pieces on hunting, fishing, and camping that began appearing in *Field & Stream* in the early 1950s.

In 1952, the magazine inaugurated Ruark's column "The Old Man and the Boy," which told the story of a remarkable friendship between a young boy and his wise grandfather. Together, the duo hunt the woods and fields of North Carolina, and fish the lakes and sea. All the while, the Old Man serves as both teacher and guide, recounting hunting and fishing lore and passing on his wisdom to his grandson. That the boy was an autobiographical portrait of Ruark is obvious; in an author's note, he writes, "Anybody who reads this book is bound to realize that I had a real fine time as a kid."

Ruark's columns were collected into book form under the same title in 1957, quickly earning a place on the bookshelves of several generations of hunters and anglers. A sequel, *The Old Man's Boy Grows Older,* soon followed, as well as a collection of Ruark's other writings on hunting, *Bring Enough Gun.*

This excerpt from *The Old Man and the Boy* depicts a deer hunt, and along the way, the tale delves deeper into the relationship between man and boy—and people and hunting—illuminating eternal truths with poignancy and eloquence.

T he week before Thanksgiving that year, one of the Old Man's best buddies came down from Maryland to spend a piece with the family, and I liked him a whole lot right from the start. Probably it was because he looked like the Old Man—ragged mustache, smoked a pipe, built sort of solid, and he treated me like I was grown up too. He was interested in 'most everything I was doing, and he admired my shotgun, and he told me a whole lot about the

Pages 68–69: *A buck searches for food amidst the morning fog as the sun rises over St. Lucie County, Florida. (Photo © Chica Stracener)*
Page 69, inset: *No buck fever here. These Minnesota hunters bagged their bucks in 1936. (Photo courtesy Minnesota Historical Society)*
Facing page: *A ten-point buck stands alert in the brambles of a raspberry patch. (Photo © Bruce Montagne)*

dogs and horses he had up on his big farm outside of Baltimore.

He and the Old Man had been friends for a whole lot of years, they had been all over the world, and they were always sitting out on the front porch, smoking and laughing quiet together over some devilment they'd been up to before I was born. I noticed they always shut up pretty quick when Miss Lottie, who was my grandma, showed up on the scene. Sometimes, when they'd come back from walking down by the river, I could smell a little ripe aroma around them that smelled an awful lot like the stuff that the Old Man kept in his room to keep the chills off him. The Old Man's friend was named Mister Howard.

They were planning to pack up the dogs and guns and a tent and go off on a camping trip for a whole week, 'way into the woods behind Allen's Creek, about fifteen miles from town. They talked about it for days, fussing around with cooking gear, and going to the store to pick up this and that, and laying out clothes. They never said a word to me; they acted as if I wasn't there at all. I was very good all the time. I never spoke at the table unless I was spoken to, and I never asked for more than I ate, and I kept pretty clean and neat, for me. My tongue was hanging out, like a thirsty hound dog's. One day I couldn't stand it any longer.

"I want to go too," I said. "You promised last summer you'd take me camping if I behaved myself and quit stealing your cigars and didn't get drowned and—"

"What do you think, Ned?" Mister Howard asked the Old Man. "Think we could use him around the camp, to do the chores and go for water and such as that?"

"I dunno," the Old Man said. "He'd probably be an awful nuisance. Probably get lost and we'd have to go look for him, or shoot one of us thinking we were a deer, or get sick or bust a leg or something. He's always breaking something. Man can't read his paper around here for the sound of snapping bones."

"Oh, hell, Ned," Mister Howard said, "let's take him. Maybe we can teach him a couple of things. We can always get Tom or Pete to run him back in the flivver, if he don't behave."

"Well," the Old Man said, grinning, "I'd sort of planned to fetch him along all along, but I was waiting to see how long it'd take him to ask."

We crowded a lot of stuff into that old tin Liz. Mister Howard and the Old Man and me and two bird dogs and two hound dogs and a sort of fice dog who was death on squirrels and a big springer spaniel who was death on ducks. Then there were Tom and Pete, two kind of half-Indian backwoods boys who divided their year into four parts. They fished in the summer and hunted in the fall. They made corn liquor in the winter and drank it up in the spring. They were big, dark, lean men, very quiet and strong. Both of them always wore hip boots, in the town and in the woods, on the water or in their own back yards. Both of them worked for the Old Man when the fishing season was on and the pogies were running in big, red, fatbacked schools. They knew just about everything about dogs and woods and water and game that I wanted to know.

The back seat was full of dogs and people and cooking stuff and guns. There were a couple of tents strapped on top of the Liz, a big one and a small one. That old tin can sounded like a boiler factory when we ran over the bumps in the corduroy clay road. I didn't say anything as we rode along. I was much too excited; and anyhow, I figured they might decide to send me back home.

It took us a couple of hours of bumping through the long, yellow savanna-land hills before we came up to a big pond, about five hundred yards from a swamp, or branch, with a clear creek running through it. We drove the flivver up under a group of three big water oaks and parked her. The Old Man had camped there lots before, he said. There was a cleared-out space of clean ground about fifty yards square between the trees and the branch. And there was a small fireplace, or what had been a small fireplace, of big stones. They were scattered around now, all over the place. A flock of tin cans and some old bottles and such had been tossed off in the bush.

"Damned tourists," the Old Man muttered, unloading some tin pots and pans from the back of the car. "Come in here to a man's best place and leave it looking like a hogwallow. You, son, go pick up those cans and bury them some place out of my sight. Then

come back here and help with the tents."

By the time I finished collecting the mess and burying it, the men had the tents laid out flat on the ground, the flaps fronting south, because there was a pretty stiff northerly wind working, and facing in the direction of the pond. Tom crawled under the canvas with one pole and a rope, and Pete lifted the front end with another pole and the other end of the rope. Mister Howard was behind with the end of Tom's rope and a peg and a maul. The Old Man was at the front with the end of Pete's rope and another stake and maul. The boys in the tent gave a heave, set the posts, and the two old men hauled taut on the ropes and took a couple of turns around the pegs.

The tent hung there like a blanket on a clothesline until Tom and Pete scuttled out and pegged her out stiff and taut from the sides. They pounded the pegs deep into the dirt, so that the lines around the notches were clean into the earth. It was a simple tent, just a canvas V with flaps fore and aft, but enough to keep the wet out. The other one went up the same way.

We didn't have any bedrolls in those days, or cots either. The Old Man gave me a hatchet and sent me off to chop the branches of the longleaf pine saplings that grew all around—big green needles a foot and a half long. While I was gone he cut eight pine stakes off an old stump, getting a two-foot stake every time he slivered off the stump, and then he cut four long oak saplings. He hammered the stakes into the ground inside the tent until he had a wide rectangle about six by eight feet. Then he split the tops of the stakes. He wedged two saplings into the stakes lengthwise, jamming them with the flat of the ax, and then he jammed two shorter saplings into the others, crosswise. He took four short lengths of heavy fishing cord and tied the saplings to the stakes, at each of the four corners, until he had a framework, six inches off the ground.

"Gimme those pine boughs," he said to me, "and go fetch more until I tell you to stop."

The Old Man took the fresh-cut pine branches, the resin still oozing stickily off the bright yellow slashes, and started shingling them, butt to the

*Their images reflected in the ice, three whitetail does high-step across a semifrozen stretch of the Mississippi River. (Photo © Bill Marchel)*

Above: *A herd of whitetails charges through a flooded Louisiana river. (Photo © Erwin and Peggy Bauer)*
Facing page: *A large Texas buck crowned with a majestic rack of antlers. (Photo © Steve Bentsen)*

ground. He overlapped the needles like shingles on a house, always with the leaf end up and the branch end down to the ground. It took him about fifteen minutes, but when he finished he had a six-by-eight mattress of the spicy-smelling pine boughs. Then he took a length of canvas tarpaulin and arranged it neatly over the top. There were little grommet holes in each of the four corners, and he pegged the canvas tight over the tops of the saplings that confined the pine boughs. When he was through, you could hit it with your hand and it was springy but firm.

"That's a better mattress than your grandma's got," the Old Man said, grinning over his shoulder as he hit the last lick with the ax. "All it needs is one blanket under you and one over you. You're off the ground, and dry as a bone, with pine needles to smell while you dream. It's just big enough for two men and a boy. The boy gets to sleep in the middle, and he better not thrash around and snore."

By the time he was through and I had spread the blankets, Tom and Pete had made themselves a bed in the other tent, just the same way. The whole op-

eration didn't take half an hour from stopping the car until both tents and beds were ready.

While we were building the beds Mister Howard had strung a line between a couple of trees and had tied a loop in the long leash of each dog, running the loop around the rope between the trees and jamming it with a square knot. The dogs had plenty of room to move in, but not enough to tangle up with each other, and not enough to start to fight when they got fed. They had just room enough between each dog to be sociable and growl at each other without starting a big rumpus. Pretty soon they quit growling and lay down quietly.

We had two big canvas water bags tied to the front of the flivver, and the Old Man gestured at them. "Boys have to handle the water detail in a man's camp," he said. "Go on down to the branch and fill 'em up at that little spillway. Don't roil up the water. Just stretch the necks and let the water run into the bags."

I walked down through the short yellow grass and the sparkleberry bushes to the branch, where you could hear the stream making little chuckling noises as it burbled over the rocks in its sandy bed. It was clear, brown water, and smelled a little like the crushed ferns and the wet brown leaves around it and in it. When I got back, I could hear the sound of axes off in a scrub-oak thicket, where Tom and Pete had gone to gather wood. Mister Howard was sorting out the guns, and the Old Man was puttering around with the stones where the fire marks were. He didn't look up.

"Take the hatchet and go chop me some kindling off that lighterd-knot stump," he said. "Cut 'em small, and try not to hit a knot and chop off a foot. Won't need much, 'bout an armful."

When I got back with kindling, Tom and Pete were coming out of the scrub-oak thicket with huge, heaping armfuls of old dead branches and little logs as big as your leg. They stacked them neatly at a respectable distance from where the Old Man had just about finished his oven. It wasn't much of an oven—just three sides of stones, with one end open and a few stones at intervals in the middle. I dumped the kindling down by him, and he scruffed up an old newspaper and rigged the fat pine on top, in a little sharp-pointed tepee over the crumpled paper.

He put some small sticks of scrubby oak crisscross over the fat pine, and then laid four small logs, their ends pointing in to each other until they made a cross, over the stones and over the little wigwam of kindling he had erected. Then he touched a match to the paper, and it went up in a poof. The blaze licked into the resiny lightwood, which roared and crackled into flame, soaring in yellow spurts up to the other, stouter kindling and running eager tongues around the lips of the logs. In five minutes it was roaring, reflecting bright red against the stones.

The Old Man got up and kicked his feet out to get the cramp out of his knees. It was just on late dusk. The sun had gone down, red over the hill, and the night chill was coming. You could see the fog rising in snaking wreaths out of the branch. The frogs were beginning to talk, and the night birds were stirring down at the edge of the swamp. A whippoor-will tuned up.

"'Bout time we had a little snort, Howard," the Old Man said. "It's going to be chilly. Pete! Fetch the jug!"

Pete ducked into his tent and came out with a half-gallon jug of brown corn liquor. Tom produced four tin cups from the nest of cooking utensils at the foot of the tree on which they had hung the water bags, and each man poured a half-measure of the whisky into his cup. I reckoned there must have been at least half a pint in each cup. Tom got one of the water bags and tipped it into the whisky until each man said, "Whoa." They drank and sighed. The Old Man cocked an eye at me and said, "This is for when you're bigger."

They had another drink before the fire had burned down to coal, with either Tom or Pete getting up to push the burning ends of the logs closer together. When they had a solid bed of coal glowing in the center of the stones, the Old Man heaved himself up and busied himself with a frying pan and some paper packages. He stuck a coffee pot off to one side, laid out five tin plates, dribbled coffee into the pot, hollered for me to fetch some water to pour into the pot, started carving up a loaf of bread, and slapped some big thick slices of ham into the frying pan.

When the ham was done, he put the slices, one by one, into the tin plates, which had warmed through from the fire, and laid slices of bread into the bubbling ham grease. Then he broke egg after egg onto the bread, stirred the whole mess into a thick bread-egg-and-ham-grease omelet, chopped the omelet into sections, and plumped each section onto a slice of ham. He poured the steaming coffee into cups, jerked his thumb at a can of condensed milk and a paper bag of sugar, and announced that dinner was served.

He had to cook the same mess three more times and refill the coffee pot before we quit eating. It was black dark, with no moon, when we lay back in front of the fire. The owls were talking over the whippoor-wills, and the frogs were making an awful fuss.

The Old Man gestured at me. "Take the dirty dishes and the pans down to the branch and wash 'em," he said. "Do it now, before the grease sets. You won't need soap. Use sand. Better take a flashlight, and look out for snakes."

I was scared to go down there by myself, through that long stretch of grass and trees leading to the swamp, but I would have died before admitting it.

*A doe peers out from its hiding place within a stand of tall grass. (Photo © Jamie Ruggles)*

The trees made all sorts of funny ghostly figures, and the noises were louder. When I got back, Mister Howard was feeding the dogs and the Old Man had pushed more logs on the fire.

"You better go to bed, son," the Old Man said. "Turn in in the middle. We'll be up early in the morning, and maybe get us a turkey."

I pulled off my shoes and crawled under the blanket. I heard the owl hoot again and the low mutter from the men, giant black shapes sitting before the fire. The pine-needle mattress smelled wonderful under me, and the blankets were warm. The fire pushed its heat into the tent, and I was as full of food as a tick. Just before I died I figured that tomorrow had to be heaven.

It was awful cold when the Old Man hit me a lick in the ribs with his elbow and said, "Get up, boy, and fix that fire." The stars were still up, frosty in the sky, and a wind was whistling round the corners of the tent. You could see the fire flicker just a mite against the black background of the swamp. Mister Howard was still snoring on his side of the pine-needle-canvas bed, and I remember that his mustache was riffling, like marsh grass in the wind. Over in Tom and Pete's tent you could hear two breeds of snores. One was squeaky, and the other sounded like a bull caught in a bob-wire fence. I crawled out from under the covers, shivering, and jumped into my hunting boots, which were stiff and very cold. Everything else I owned I'd slept in.

The fire was pretty feeble. It had simmered down into gray ash, which was swirling loosely in the morning breeze. There was just a little red eye blinking underneath the fine talcumy ashes. After kicking some of the ashes aside with my boot, I put a couple of lightwood knots on top of the little chunk of glowing coal, and then I dragged some live-oak logs over the top of the lightwood and waited for her to catch. She caught, and the tiny teeth of flame opened wide to eat the oak. In five minutes I had a blaze going, and I was practically in it. It was mean cold that morning.

When the Old Man saw the fire dancing, he woke up Mister Howard and reached for his pipe first and his boots next. Then he reached for the bottle and poured himself a dram in a tin cup. He shuddered some when the dram went down.

*A quartet of whitetail does and fawns keeps a wary watch. (Photo © Jamie Ruggles)*

"I heartily disapprove of drinking in the morning," he said. "Except some mornings. It takes a man past sixty to know whether he can handle his liquor good enough to take a nip in the morning. Howard?"

"I'm past sixty too," Mister Howard said. "Pass the jug."

Tom and Pete were coming out of the other tent, digging their knuckles into sleepy eyes. Pete went down to the branch and fetched a bucket of water, and everybody washed their faces out of the bucket. Then Pete went to the fire and slapped some ham into the pan and some eggs into the skillet, set some bread to toasting, and put the coffee pot on. Breakfast didn't take long. We had things to do that day.

After the second cup of coffee—I can still taste that coffee, with the condensed milk sweet and curdled on the top and the coffee itself tasting of branch water and wood smoke—we got up and started sorting out the guns.

"This is a buckshot day," the Old Man said, squinting down the barrel of his pump gun. "I think we better get us a deer today. Need meat in the camp, and maybe we can blood the boy. Tom, Pete, you all drive the branch. Howard, we'll put the boy on a stand where a buck is apt to amble by, and then you and I will kind of drift around according to where the noise seems headed. One, t'other of us ought to get a buck. This crick is populous with deer."

The Old Man paused to light his pipe, and then he turned around and pointed the stem at me.

"You, boy," he said. "By this time you know a lot about guns, but you don't know a lot about guns and deer together. Many a man loses his wits when he sees a big ol' buck bust out of the bushes with a rockin' chair on his head. Trained hunters shoot each other. They get overexcited and just bang away into the bushes. *Mind* what I say. A deer ain't a deer unless it's got horns on its head and you can see all of it at once. We don't shoot does and we don't shoot spike bucks and we don't shoot each other. There ain't no sense to shootin' a doe or a young'un. One buck can service hundreds of does, and one doe will breed you a mess of deer. If you shoot a young'un, you haven't got much meat, and no horns at all, and you've kept him from breedin' to make more deer for you to shoot. If you shoot a man, they'll likely hang you, and if the man is me I will be awful gol-damned annoyed and come back to ha'nt you.

You mind that gun, and don't pull a trigger until you can see what it is and *where* it is. *Mind*, I say."

Tom and Pete picked up their pump guns and loaded them. They pushed the load lever down so there'd be no shell in the chamber, but only in the magazine. The Old Man looked at my little gun and said, "Don't bother to load it until you get on the stand. You ain't likely to see anything to shoot for an hour or so."

Tom and Pete went over to where we had the dogs tethered on a line strung between two trees, and he unleashed the two hounds, Bell and Blue. Bell was black-and-tan and all hound. Blue was a kind of a sort of dog. He had some plain hound, some Walker hound, and some bulldog and a little beagle and a smidgen of pointer in him. He was ticked blue and brown and black and yellow and white. He looked as if somebody spilled the eggs on the checkered tablecloth. But he was a mighty dandy deer dog, or so they said. Old Sam Watts, across the street, used to say there wasn't no use trying to tell Blue anything, because Blue had done forgot more than you knew and just got annoyed when you tried to tell him his business.

Tom snapped a short lead on Blue, and Pete snapped another one on Bell. They shouldered their guns and headed up the branch, against the wind. We let 'em walk, while the Old Man and Mister Howard puttered around, like old people and most women will. Drives a boy crazy. What I wanted to do was go and shoot myself a deer. *Now*.

After about ten minutes the Old Man picked up his gun and said, "Let's go." We walked about half a mile down the swamp's edge. The light had come now, lemon-colored, and the fox squirrels were beginning to chase each other through the gum trees. We spied one old possum in a persimmon tree, hunched into a ball and making out like nobody knew he was there. We heard a turkey gobble away over yonder somewheres, and we could hear the doves beginning to moan—*oooh—oohoo —oooooh.*

All the little birds started to squeak and chirp and twitter at each other. The dew was staunchly stiff on the grass and on the sparkleberry and gallberry bushes. It was still cold, but getting warmer, and breakfast had settled down real sturdy in my stomach. Rabbits jumped out from under our feet. We stepped smack onto a covey of quail just working its

*Outlined by first light, a whitetail buck strolls through autumn grasses. (Photo © Len Rue, Jr.)*

way out of the swamp, and they like to have scared me to death when they busted up under our feet. There was a lot going on in that swamp that morning.

We turned into the branch finally, and came up to a track that the Old Man said was a deer run. He looked around and spied a stump off to one side, hidden by a tangle of dead brush. From the stump you could see clear for about fifty yards in a sort of accidental arena.

"Go sit on that stump, boy," the Old Man said. "You'll hear the dogs after a while, and if a deer comes down this branch he'll probably bust out there, where that trail comes into the open, because there ain't any other way he can cross it without leaving the swamp. Don't let the dogs fool you into not paying attention. When you hear 'em a mile away, the chances are that deer will be right in your lap. Sometimes they travel as much as two miles ahead of the dogs, just slipping along, not running; just slipping and sneaking on their little old quiet toes. And stay still. A deer'll run right over you if you stay still and the smell is away from him. But if you wink an eye, he can see it two hundred yards off, and will go the other way."

I sat down on the stump. The Old Man and Mis-

ter Howard went off, and I could hear them chatting quietly as they disappeared. I looked all around me. Nothing much was going on now, except a couple of he-squirrels were having a whale of a fight over my head, racing across branches and snarling squirrel cuss words at each other. A chickadee was standing on its head in a bush and making chickadee noises. A redheaded woodpecker was trying to cut a live-oak trunk in half with his bill. A rain crow—a kind of cuckoo, it is—was making dismal noises off behind me in the swamp, and a big old yellow hammer was swooping and dipping from tree to tree.

There were some robins hopping around on a patch of burnt ground, making conversation with each other. Crows were cawing, and two doves looped in to sit in a tree and chuckle at each other. A towhee was scratching and making more noise than a herd of turkeys, and some catbirds were meowing in the low bush while a big, sassy old mocker was imitating them kind of sarcastically. Anybody who says woods are quiet is crazy. You learn how to listen. The Tower of Babel was a study period alongside of woods in the early morning.

It is wonderful to smell the morning. Anybody who's been around the woods knows that morning smells one way, high noon another, dusk still another, and night most different of all, if only because the skunks smell louder at night. Morning smells fresh and flowery and little-breezy, and dewy and spanking new. Noon smells hot and a little dusty and sort of sleepy, when the breeze has died and the heads begin to droop and anything with any sense goes off into the shade to take a nap. Dusk smells scary. It is getting colder and everybody is going home tired for the day, and you can smell the turpentine scars on the trees and the burnt-off ground and the bruised ferns and the rising wind. You can hear the folding-up, I'm-finished-for-the-day sounds all around, including the colored boys whistling to prove they ain't scared when they drive the cows home. And in the night you can smell the fire and the warm blankets and the coffee a-boil, and you can even smell the stars. I know that sounds silly, but on a cool, clear, frosty night the stars have a smell, or so it seems when you are young and acutely conscious of everything bigger than a chigger.

This was as nice a smelling morning as I can remember. It smelled like it was going to work into a real fine-smelling day. The sun was up pretty high now and was beginning to warm the world. The dew was starting to dry, because the grass wasn't clear wet any more but just had little drops on top, like a kid with a runny nose. I sat on the stump for about a half-hour, and then I heard the dogs start, a mile or more down the swamp. Bell picked up the trail first, and she sounded as if church had opened for business. Then Blue came in behind her, loud as an organ, their two voices blending—fading sometimes, getting stronger, changing direction always.

Maybe you never heard a hound in the woods on a frosty fall morning, with the breeze light, the sun heating up in the sky, and the "aweful" expectancy that something big was going to happen to you. There aren't many things like it. When the baying gets closer and closer and still closer to you, you feel as if maybe you're going to explode if something doesn't happen quick. And when the direction changes and the dogs begin to fade, you feel so sick you want to throw up.

But Bell and Blue held the scent firmly now, and the belling was clear and steady. The deer was moving steady and straight, not trying to circle and fool the dogs, but honestly running. And the noise was coming straight down the branch, with me on the other end of it.

The dogs had come so close that you could hear them panting between their bays, and once or twice one of them quit sounding and broke into a yip-yap of barks. I thought I could hear a little tippety-tappety noise ahead of them, in between the belling and the barking, like mice running through paper or a rabbit hopping through dry leaves. I kept my eyes pinned onto where the deer path opened into the clearing. The dogs were so close that I could hear them crash.

All of a sudden there was a flash of brown and two does, flop-eared, with two half-grown fawns skipped out of the brush, stopped dead in front of me, looked me smack in the face, and then gave a tremendous leap that carried them halfway across the clearing. They bounced again, white tails carried high, and disappeared into the branch behind me.

*In a morning fog, a whitetail buck stretches for food from an overhanging tree branch. (Photo © Steve Bentsen)*

As I turned to watch them go there was another crash ahead and the buck tore through the clearing like a race horse. He wasn't jumping. This boy was running like the wind, with his horns laid back against his spine and his ears pinned by the breeze he was making. The dogs were right behind him. He had held back to tease the dogs into letting his family get a start, and now that they were out of the way he was pouring on the coal and heading for home

I had a gun with me and the gun was loaded. I suppose it would have fired if the thought had occurred to me to pull the trigger. The thought never occurred. I just watched that big buck deer run, with my mouth open and my eyes popped out of my head.

The dogs tore out of the bush behind the buck, baying out their brains and covering the ground in leaps. Old Blue looked at me as he flashed past and curled his lip. He looked as if he were saying, "This is man's work, and what is a boy doing here, spoiling my labor?" Then he dived into the bush behind the buck.

I sat there on the stump and began to shake and tremble. About five minutes later there was one shot, a quarter-mile down the swamp. I sat on the stump. In about half an hour Tom and Pete came up to my clearing.

"What happened to the buck?" Pete said. "Didn't he come past here? I thought I was going to run him right over you."

"He came past, all right," I said, feeling sick-mean, "but I never shot. I never even thought about it until he was gone. I reckon you all ain't ever going to take me along any more." My lip was shaking and now I *was* about to cry.

Tom walked over and hit me on top of the head with the flat of his hand. "Happens to everybody," he said. "Grown men and boys, both, they all get buck fever. Got to do it once before you get over it. Forget it. I seen Pete here shoot five times at a buck big as a horse last year, and missed him with all five."

There were some footsteps in the branch where the deer had disappeared, and in a minute Mister Howard and the Old Man came out, with the dogs leashed and panting.

*Appearing out of the morning mist, a whitetail buck with a healthy rack peers from a stand of grass. (Photo © Robert McKemie/Earth Images)*

Above: *Almost lost in the light of sunset, a Texas buck with velvety antlers moves into a clearing. (Photo © Steve Bentsen)*
Facing page: *Topped by a huge rack, a buck watches from the cover of a goldenrod field near a fallen oak. (Photo © Bill Marchel)*

"Missed him clean," the Old Man said cheerfully. "Had one whack at him no farther'n thirty yards and missed him slick as a whistle. That's the way it is, but there's always tomorrow. Let's us go shoot some squirrels for the pot, and we'll rest the dogs and try again this evenin'. You *see* him, boy?"

"I *saw* him," I said. "And I ain't ever going to *forget* him."

We went back to camp and tied up the hounds. We unleashed the fice dog, Jackie, the little sort of yellow fox terrier kind of nothing dog with prick ears and a sharp fox's face and a thick tail that curved up over his back. I was going with Pete to shoot some squirrels while the old gentlemen policed up the camp, rested, took a couple of drinks, and started to prepare lunch. It was pretty late in the morning for squirrel hunting, but this swamp wasn't hunted

much. While I had been on the deer stand that morning the swamp was alive with them—mostly big fox squirrels, huge old fellers with a lot of black on their gray-and-white hides.

"See you don't get squirrel fever," the Old Man hollered over his shoulder as Pete and I went down to the swamp. "Else we'll all starve to death. I'm about fresh out of ham and eggs."

"Don't pay no 'tention to him, son," Pete told me. "He's a great kidder."

"Hell with him," I said. "He missed the deer, didn't he? At least *I* didn't miss him."

"That's right," Pete agreed genially. "You got to shoot at 'em to miss 'em."

I looked quick and sharp at Pete. He didn't seem to be teasing me. A cigarette was hanging off the corner of his lip, and his lean, brown, Injun-looking face was completely straight. Then we heard Jackie,

yip-yapping in a querulous bark, as if somebody had just insulted him by calling him a dog.

"Jackie done treed hisself a squirrel," Pete said. "Advantage of a dog like Jackie is that when the squirrels all come down to the ground to feed, ol' Jackie rousts 'em up and makes 'em head for the trees. Then he makes so much noise he keeps the squirrel interested while we go up and wallop away at him. Takes two men to hunt squirrels this way. Jackie barks. I go around to the other side of the tree. Squirrel sees me and moves. That's when you shoot him, when he slides around on your side. Gimme your gun."

"Why?" I asked. "What'll I use to shoot the—"

"*Mine*," Pete answered. "You ain't going to stand there and tell me you're gonna use a shotgun on a squirrel? Anybody can hit a pore little squirrel with a shotgun. Besides, shotgun shells cost a nickel apiece."

I noticed Pete's gun for the first time. He had left his pump gun in camp and had a little bolt-action .22. He took my shotgun from me and handed me the .22 and a handful of cartridges.

"'Nother thing you ought to know," Pete said as we walked up to the tree, a big blue gum under which Jackie seemed to be going mad, "is that when you're hunting for the pot you don't belong to make much more noise with guns than is necessary. You go booming off a shotgun, blim-blam, and you spook ever'thing in the neighborhood. A .22 don't make no more noise than a stick crackin', and agin the wind you can't hear it more'n a hundred yards or thereabouts. Best meat gun in the world, a straight-shootin' .22, because it don't make no noise and don't spoil the meat. Look up yonder, on the fourth fork. There's your dinner. A big ol' fox squirrel, near-about black all over."

The squirrel was pasted to the side of the tree. Pete walked around, and the squirrel moved with him. When Pete was on the other side, making quite a lot of noise, the squirrel shifted back around to my side. He was peeping at Pete, but his shoulders and back and hind legs were on my side. I raised the little .22 and plugged him between the shoulders. He came down like a sack of rocks. Jackie made a dash for him,

*With its white tail held high, a mature buck seems to prance through the morning sunshine. (Photo © Erwin and Peggy Bauer)*

grabbed him by the back, shook him once and broke his spine, and sort of spit him out on the ground. The squirrel was dang near as big as Jackie.

Pete and I hunted squirrels for an hour or so, and altogether we shot ten. Pete said that was enough for five people for a couple of meals, and there wasn't no sense to shootin' if the meat had to spoil. "We'll have us some venison by tomorrow, anyways," he said. "One of us is bound to git one. You shot real nice with that little bitty gun," he said. "She'll go where you hold her, won't she?"

I felt pretty good when we went into camp and the Old Man, Mister Howard, and Tom looked up inquiringly. Pete and I started dragging fox squirrels out of our hunting coats, and the ten of them made quite a sizable pile.

"Who shot the squirrels?" the Old Man asked genially. "The dog?"

"Sure," Pete grinned. "Dog's so good we've taught him to shoot, too. We jest set down on a log, give Jackie the gun, and sent him off into the branch on his lonesome. We're planning to teach him to skin 'em and cook 'em, right after lunch. This is the best dog I ever see. Got more sense than people."

"Got more sense than *some* people," the Old Man grunted. "Come and git it, boy, and after lunch you and Jackie can skin the squirrels."

The lunch was a lunch I loved then and still love, which is why I'm never going to be called one of those epicures. This was a country hunting lunch, Carolina style. We had Vienna sausages and sardines, rat cheese, gingersnaps and dill pickles and oysterettes and canned salmon, all cold except the coffee that went with it, and that was hot enough to scald clean down to your shoes. It sounds horrible, but I don't know anything that tastes so good together as Vienna sausages and sardines and rat cheese and gingersnaps. Especially if you've been up since before dawn and walked ten miles in the fresh air.

After lunch we stretched out in the shade and took a little nap. Along about two I woke up, and so did Pete and Tom, and the three of us started to skin the squirrels. It's not much trouble, if you know how. Pete and I skinned 'em and Tom cleaned and dressed 'em. I'd pick up a squirrel by the head, and Pete would take his hind feet. We'd stretch him tight, and Pete would slit him down the stomach and along the legs

as far as the feet. Then he'd shuck him like an ear of corn, pulling the hide toward the head until it hung over his head like a cape and the squirrel was naked. Then he'd just chop off the head, skin and all, and toss the carcass to Tom.

Tom made a particular point about cutting the little castor glands. Squirrel with the musk glands out is as tasty as any meat I know, but unless you take out those glands an old he-squirrel is as musky as a billy goat, and tastes like a billy goat smells. Tom cut up the carcasses and washed them clean, and I proceeded to bury the heads, hides, and guts.

The whole job didn't take forty-five minutes with the three of us working. We put the pieces of clean red meat in a covered pot, and then woke up the Old Man and Mister Howard. We were going deer hunting again.

The dogs had rested too; they had had half a can of salmon each and about three hours' snooze. It was beginning to cool off when Tom and Pete put Blue and Bell on walking leashes and we struck off for another part of the swamp, which made a Y from the main swamp and had a lot of water in it. It was a cool swamp, and Tom and Pete figured that the deer would be lying up there from the heat of the day, and about ready to start stirring out to feed a little around dusk.

I was in the process of trying to think about just how long forever was when the hounds started to holler real close. They seemed to be coming straight down the crick off to my right, and the crick's banks were very open and clear, apart from some sparkleberry and gallberry bushes. The *whoo-whooing* got louder and louder. The dogs started to growl and bark, just letting off a *woo-woo* once in a while, and I could hear a steady swishing in the bushes.

Then I could see what made the swishing. It was a buck, a big one. He was running steadily and seriously through the low bush. He had horns—my Lord, but did he have horns! It looked to me like he had a dead tree lashed to his head. I slipped off the safety catch and didn't move. The buck came straight at me, the dogs going crazy behind him.

The buck came down the water's edge, and when he got to about fifty yards I stood up and threw the gun up to my face. He kept coming and I let him come. At about twenty-five yards he suddenly saw

*Its antlers still in velvet, a Long Island buck stands amid a field of bowed-over grass. (Photo © Ann Littlejohn)*

me, snorted, and leaped to his left as if somebody had unsnapped a spring in him. I forgot he was a deer. I shot at him as you'd lead a duck or a quail on a quartering shot—plenty of lead ahead of his shoulder.

I pulled the trigger—for some odd reason shooting the choke barrel—right in the middle of a spring that had him six feet off the ground and must have been wound up to send him twenty yards, into the bush and out of my life. The gun said *boom!* but I didn't hear it. The gun kicked but I didn't feel it. All I saw was that this monster came down out of the sky like I'd shot me an airplane. He came down flat, turning completely over and landing on his back, and he never wiggled.

The dogs came up ferociously and started to grab him, but they had sense and knew he didn't need any extra grabbing. I'd grabbed him real good, with about three ounces of No. 1 buckshot in a choke barrel. I had busted his shoulder and busted his neck and dead-centered his heart. I had let him get so close that you could practically pick the wads out of his shoulder. This was *my* buck. Nobody else had shot at him. Nobody else had seen him but me. Nobody had advised or helped. This monster was mine.

And monster was right. He was huge, they told me later, for a Carolina whitetail. He had fourteen points on his rack, and must have weighed nearly 150 pounds undressed. He was beautiful gold on his top and dazzling white on his underneath, and his little black hoofs were clean. The circular tufts of hair on his legs, where the scent glands are, were bright russet and stiff and spiky. His horns were as clean as if they'd been scrubbed with a wire brush, gnarled and evenly forked and the color of planking on a good boat that's just been holystoned to where the decks sparkle.

I had him all to myself as he lay there in the aromatic, crushed ferns—all by myself, like a boy alone in a big cathedral of oaks and cypress in a vast swamp where the doves made sobbing sounds and the late birds walked and talked in the sparkleberry bush. The dogs came up and lay down. Old Blue laid his muzzle on the big buck's back. Bell came over and licked my face and wagged her tail, like she was saying, "You did real good, boy." Then she lay down and put her face right on the deer's rump.

This was our deer, and no damn bear or anything else was going to take it away from us. We were a team, all right, me and Bell and Blue.

I couldn't know then that I was going to grow up and shoot elephants and lions and rhinos and things. All I knew then was that I was the richest boy in the world as I sat there in the crushed ferns and stroked the silky hide of my first buck deer, patting his horns and smelling how sweet he smelled and admiring how pretty he looked. I cried a little bit inside about how lovely he was and how I felt about him. I guess that was just reaction, like being sick twenty-five years later when I shot my first African buffalo.

I was still patting him and patting the dogs when Tom and Pete came up one way and the Old Man and Mister Howard came up from another way. What a wonderful thing it was when you are a kid, to have four huge, grown men—everything is bigger when you are a boy—come roaring up out of the woods to see you sitting by your first big triumph. "Smug" is a word I learned a lot later. Smug was modest for what I felt then.

"Well," the Old Man said, trying not to grin.

"Well," Mister Howard said.

"Boy done shot hisself a horse with horns," Pete said, as proud for me as if I had just learned how to make bootleg liquor.

"Shot him pretty good, too," Tom said. "Deer musta been standing still, boy musta been asleep, woke up, and shot him in self-defense."

"Was not, either," I started off to say, and then saw that all four men were laughing.

They had already checked the sharp scars where the buck had jumped, and they knew I had shot him on the fly. Then Pete turned the buck over and cut open his belly. He tore out the paunch and ripped it open. It was full of green stuff and awful smelly gunk. All four men let out a whoop and grabbed me. Pete held the paunch and the other men stuck my head right into—blood, guts, green gunk, and all. It smelled worse than anything I ever smelled. I was bloody and full of partly digested deer fodder from my head to my belt.

"That," the Old Man said as I swabbed the awful mess off me and dived away to stick my head in the crick, "makes you a grown man. You have been blooded, boy, and any time you miss a deer from now on we cut off your shirt tail. It's a very good buck, son," he said softly, "one of which you can be very, very proud."

*Silhouetted against the sunlight shining through the clouds, a buck and doe stand atop Big Bend National Park, Texas. (Photo © Erwin and Peggy Bauer)*

Tom and Pete cut a long sapling, made slits in the deer's legs behind the cartilage of his knees, stuck the sapling through the slits, and slung the deer up on their backs. They were sweating him through the swamp when suddenly the Old Man turned to Mister Howard and said, "Howard, if you feel up to it, we might just as well go get *our* deer and lug him into camp. He ain't but a quarter-mile over yonder, and I don't want the wildcats working on him in that tree."

"What deer?" I demanded. "You didn't shoot this afternoon, and you missed the one you—"

The Old Man grinned and made a show of lighting his pipe. "I didn't miss him, son," he said. "I just didn't want to give you an inferiority complex on your first deer. If you hadn't of shot this one—and he's a lot better'n mine—I was just going to leave him in the tree and say nothing about him at all. Shame to waste a deer; but it's a shame to waste a boy, too."

I reckon that's when I quit being a man. I just opened my mouth and bawled. Nobody laughed at me, either.

# SWAMP BUCK

## by Frances Hamerstrom

Frances Hamerstrom is a former debutante and fashion model who also happens to be a proficient deer hunter. She learned to hunt as a teenager, bagging ducks on the sly, as it was not the thing to do for a well-bred young lady. As she grew older, she brought her passion out in the open, and she has hunted every season since 1920.

Her insightful and fun book, *Is She Coming Too? Memoirs of a Lady Hunter,* tells of the trials and tribulations of being a woman who hunts. She recounts an early date to go hunting with a Harvard boy whom she had a crush on; he stood her up, as *he* thought the weather was too inclement. In the story reprinted here, she describes deer hunting with her husband, Frederick, and the swamp buck that got away.

Just get a job with the conservation department—hunt and fish the rest of your life. Well I did get a job with the Wisconsin Conservation Department in 1950 and hunting—especially deer hunting—was swiftly curtailed. We worked at checking stations during the deer season, so Frederick and I usually got little time off for hunting, and we tended to be in a totally unfamiliar part of the state with no chance to do even the most preliminary scouting.

Each year my hopes followed the same sequence. When sighting in my rifle, a .250-3000, I dreamed of shooting an enormous swamp buck with a rack that would make everyone marvel. After a few hours afield, I was ready to settle for any legal deer. Wisconsin had just permitted a doe season. (Some purists feel that only yellowbellies would shoot a doe, but I confess a doe would have made me very happy.) After a few more hours, it was plain to me that still hunting (stalking) wasn't getting me anywhere, but I usually managed to pick up a blood trail. Well, I suppose you know what I was hoping by now: I was hoping to find a dead deer lying at the end of the trail.

I don't know why I should be telling anybody my secret thoughts. Right now I would like to make one thing perfectly clear: never in my whole life did I *start* the day so depleted in spirit that I longed for a trail leading to somebody else's dead deer.

The Department usually sent us to a deer check station where there was a goodly concentration of hunters. Sometimes we were allowed to hunt the first three hours of the season before arriving at our assigned station. One year we hunted with Bob McCabe, a merry com-

*A robust whitetail buck. (Photo © Art Wolfe)*

BUCK FEVER / 98

panion of Irish descent. Shots rang out from all directions as the season opened at dawn. Shooting for the party was looked down on by our bunch. We considered it more gentlemanly for each person to get his own deer. There was a slight lull after the opening barrage and then somebody shouted, "I got one! I got two! I got *three!*" McCabe's unmistakable Irish voice came next, echoing through the pin oaks, "I got four! I got five! I got *six!*"

McCabe seemed to thrive in crowds. I usually had to beg Frederick to come deer hunting because he wants the woods pristine—just for us. Bob's wife, Marie, went bird hunting with him and kept up his breakneck pace through the thickest of brush, but she never seemed to go deer hunting. I led up to the subject one day and she said, "Fran, I used to worry.

"You read about all those accidents in deer season.

"I used to worry when Bob went . . .

"But then," Marie added, "we got a deep freeze."

One year Os Mattson guided us in his home terrain near Black River Falls. Os put us each on a stand and told us to stay put.

Os got a shot with his borrowed Egyptian. He was so startled by all the smoke from the black powder that we never heard why he didn't get his deer.

Frederick was also shooting a borrowed rifle. He had almost refused to come. He was deep into a research project on Central Wisconsin deer. (He predicted the Wisconsin eruption as early as 1940.) After checking on populations and evaluating over-browsing he figured the knowledge so obtained gave him unfair advantage. To come right out with it: he figured getting his deer would be too easy!

Frederick finally came on the Black River Falls hunt not because he wanted to, but to please Os and me. I feared that it would probably be the last time in his life that anybody was going to persuade him to indulge in anything so banal as deer hunting in Wisconsin.

Frederick prefers still hunting, but he can sit absolutely motionless on a stand. My man just never fidgets.

The number of deer in that section near Black River Falls was astounding. Their hoofs kept pummeling like horses' chased around in a pasture. Frederick chose the intersection of two major run-

ways, and bided his time. Does came tripping along cracking twigs and otherwise drawing attention to themselves. A few minor bucks passed within easy range. Then—just as he had figured—came a really nice one. Frederick—moving almost imperceptibly—raised his borrowed rifle, pulled the trigger, and that blessed rifle misfired.

He didn't get another shot.

Os put me on a beautiful stand. It was on a tiny oak island deep in a tamarack swamp. Sharp-edged runs had been pounded into the soft sphagnum, and the run past my stand would bring any deer into perfect position. Of course, I couldn't see any of these fine attributes of my position because it was pitch dark when Os guided me to a log, and whispered, "Sit here."

The woods were so quiet. Os treads lightly in the woods, but I could hear him depart. I got to dreaming about that big swamp buck and was well into this pleasant occupation when suddenly, somebody coughed—so close that he seemed right next to me. I couldn't shift to find another stand because it would be impolite to Os.

The guy coughed again.

I coughed back.

He coughed louder.

So did I.

What this innocent man—who was probably from the city—didn't realize was that he was up against an expert. One develops certain survival skills in the country, where the telephone company sometimes put as many as eight families on one party line. (Ours had eight.) Eight families add up to about thirty people using the same phone, and among those thirty there are bound to be at least one or two who like to use the phone for visiting, and visiting can take a long, long time.

Mind you, these eight families are your near neighbors, and it pays to get along with them. One can lift up the receiver and listen to see whether anyone is on the line. Visits go something like this:

"You don't say!"

"Uh huh."

"Well, I never!"

"What did she do then?"

"She told."

"You don't say!"

*Running with a fluid grace, a whitetail buck dashes through shallow water. (Photo © Jeanne Drake, Las Vegas, NV)*

Everybody in all eight families knew my voice because I am a Bostonian and am said to talk as though I have plums in my mouth. It wasn't long after we had the phone put in that I realized that people did not like to be interrupted while visiting. Sometimes, when I wanted to telephone, I'd lift the receiver up off and on for about forty minutes, and at last, I'd say, "Could you *please* let me use the telephone?"

"Yes, Mrs. Hamerstrom." And I had the uneasy feeling that I hadn't made a friend.

So I used coughing.

I'd lift up the receiver and hear, "You don't say!" and then I'd have a coughing fit right into the mouthpiece.

"Effie, you caught cold?"

"Nope."

Then I'd cough some more. Nobody could tell who was coughing—they couldn't even tell if it was a man or a woman.

Pretty soon the visiting was not going very well, and it just took another cough or so to hear the welcome words, "Guess I'll call you later."

The guy on my little oak island coughed again and I gave him my long, wheezy version of the telephone type. It was getting light and I knew I didn't have much time, so I tried all different types of coughing on him—except the soft type. He didn't hear any soft coughing from my direction.

At last he got up and shuffled away.

Not long after sunup, Os reappeared so silently that I barely heard him coming. "Let's get out of here. I know a place where there won't be many hunters." So Os and Frederick and I went back to the car which now had cars parked all around it like traffic near a football stadium.

Os took us to a place where we didn't see a single other hunter. Neither did we see a single deer. And yes, toward dusk I got to daydreaming about following a trail that led me—not to an excellent opportunity to shoot a big buck—but to some lost deer, just lying there dead.

After this fiasco, you can well imagine my frame of mind when Dave Seal telephoned me from Illinois and invited me to go bow hunting with him.

*A whitetail buck pauses for a drink from a cypress swamp. (Photo © Erwin and Peggy Bauer)*

"Yes, Dave."

Then I told Frederick. Dave Seal, whom we both knew to be a museum man and a skilled hunter, had invited me to go bow hunting with him!

Frederick asked. "At Necedah?"

"Yes," I gasped, "how did you know?"

"Honey, he wants you for a guide. You know that country."

"Well," I answered a little huffily, "it's better than having people say, 'Is *she* coming too?'"

Frederick tried another approach. "Have you ever shot a bow?"

"Yes."

A pained expression must have flickered over my face, because he dropped the subject. I was thinking of Camp Owaissa—a girls' camp on Cape Cod. We were to have a sports competition with another girls' camp, but some of our best athletes came down with measles. I'd had measles and I was naturally good at sports, so I was suddenly entered in the archery contest. I wore a short-sleeved middy blouse and bloomers and nobody told me about wearing an arm guard. I didn't miss the target often, but my forearm was reddish, with a tinge of purple, and somewhat bloodied up. That afternoon I entered essentially every water sport and found that swimming and diving in salt water causes a bloodied up arm to smart.

Frederick is good to me. He could tell I really wanted to go bow hunting with Dave, so he suggested that I borrow Aldo Leopold's Osage orange bow and get some practice before the season opened. Bob McCabe had inherited Aldo's bow and gladly lent it to me. Bob Ellarson lent me a quiver of arrows. The arrows were hunting arrows and I was admonished not to use them for target practice. So I practiced indoors—sort of.

Aldo's bow had a 55-pound pull. I couldn't begin to pull it. Fifty-five pounds. I could chin myself twenty times, and do push-ups till I was tired of counting them, but that bow resisted my efforts. So I went at the matter methodically. Every day I stood in front of the mirror in our living room and pulled that bow as far as I could. I am ambidextrous so when one arm got tired I switched to the other. After a few weeks I could pull that bow, slowly and evenly, and hold it pulled—steadily and with either hand. The only thing lacking was an arrow.

On opening day, Dave and I set forth. I had visualized the aroma of wintergreen underfoot, sweetfern brushing our shins, and the tranquility of the wilderness.

But bow hunting at Necedah had become popular. There were lots of cars. I found an arrow on the way to the stand where I was going to put Dave. And just as we got there a hunter came bursting forth—it seemed in a panic.

"Trouble?" Dave asked.

"Got to get to the car. Need another quiver of arrows."

"Dave, I was going to put you here. But do you mind getting your feet wet?"

Dave grinned. He had picked the right guide.

We moseyed off to the west, ploshed through some moderately cold water and found ourselves totally isolated from the rest of mankind. We each picked ourselves a stand. Mine was neatly hidden in some scrubby jackpines. My thoughts?

At that time in the morning I was still dreaming about the big swamp buck, and hadn't lowered myself to any of the lesser aspirations. That big swamp buck was about to come up out of that marsh and stand broadside . . .

He did!

I raised up and pulled that bow ever so slowly.

The buck was so close that I could almost count his eyelashes.

I held steady, but I couldn't figure out which hand to let go with . . .

I held steady, following that swamp buck as he slowly walked away from me. If I let go with the wrong hand the bow would bash me in the face. If I let go with the right hand I would, at last, kill the buck of my dreams.

I held steady—while the buck of my dreams—my swamp buck—slowly—very slowly—walked away.

*A large whitetail buck with a spider web criss-crossing its eight-point rack. (Photo © Len Rue, Jr.)*

# Chapter 4

———— ◆ ————

# THE
# BIG BUCK

*I'm always glad to see a famous buck, ram, bull or muskie get away. His legendary size or antler or horn measurements could probably never be matched by the real thing. Besides, once you've nailed him, the fun is over; the speculative record measurements have shrunk to realistic mediocrity. And next year's hunting or fishing season is not the exciting prospect it would have been had The Phantom Buck still been out there.*
*—Les Blacklock, "The Phantom Buck" from Meet My Psychiatrist, 1977*

# STAG PANTS GALAHADS

## by Sigurd F. Olson

With the landmark publication of *The Singing Wilderness* in 1956, Sigurd F. Olson distinguished himself as one of the country's most talented—and most popular—nature writers. For the next three decades, he delighted his readers with books about the rugged wilderness areas of northern Minnesota and Canada, including his classics *Listening Point, The Lonely Land,* and *Runes of the North.* His books are poetic invocations of the north country, recalling the textures of the wilderness with prose that is lucid and luminous.

Most of Olson's writing chronicles the natural history of the north, but some of his early stories and magazine articles also tell of his love for hunting and fishing. This story, first printed in *Sports Afield* magazine in November 1930, describes a typical fall hunting trip, detailing with warmth and humor the fall from grace of the author, Stag Pants Galahad.

Hey you old woods rat, wait a minute."
I turned around. It was the dean, hurrying up the street toward me. By the light in his eye, I knew something out of the ordinary was up.

"It won't be long now," was his greeting.

"What won't?" I asked stupidly.

"Come to," he said, "and take a look at this." Then with an air as momentous as though he was unveiling the only original draft of the Locarno treaty itself, he showed me a bit of yellow cardboard. Across the top, printed in bold black letters were three words and a figure. BIG GAME LICENSE 1928. I stared but said nothing.

"Better get some shells and limber up that trigger finger of yours," was his parting remark. "Another two weeks and we'll be on our way."

From that moment, my blood pressure was anything but normal. Until then, the coming of deer season had seemed rather indefinite and still too far away to worry about, but here it was, almost upon us and a million things to get done.

Everyday affairs became suddenly of a secondary importance and I wandered around,

Pages 104–105: *With his tall and wide ten-point antlers silhouetted against the sky, a large buck stands on a ridge in Minnesota. (Photo © Bill Marchel)*

Page 105, inset: *Two big bucks were a fine reward for a day of hunting along the Lake of the Woods in northern Minnesota, circa 1912. (Photo by Carl Gustaf Linde, courtesy Minnesota Historical Society)*

Facing page: *A magnificent whitetail buck during the rut. (Photo © Len Rue, Jr.)*

my brain a whirl of pack sacks, tents, rifles and grub lists. My one consolation during those trying days, was that I was not alone in my travail. As time went on, others developed the symptoms and I reveled in such intimate companionship and understanding as seldom befalls one in these sophisticated times.

One evening Glenn Powers called me over to see his new thirty-thirty. As I drew beads on all the light bulbs in the house, he told me confidentially that he had traded in his old one and only forty dollars to boot. Didn't I think it was a buy? Of course I did, though I couldn't help secretly agreeing with his otherwise understanding wife who couldn't see for the life of her why the old one wouldn't have done just as well.

Hilliard was in the midst of a new sleeping bag. I came on him one day, knee deep in duck feathers and wool batt. He was working feverishly and I knew that for him it was a race against time. To my questions he only grunted and sewed all the faster. The strain was beginning to tell.

That last week was tense with suppressed excitement. The main topic of conversation was snow. Old-timers talked of other seasons and made sage predictions about the weather and things in general. The gaily decorated windows of the hardware stores with their show of rifles, deer heads, and neatly stacked mounds of ammunition, became the meeting places for men on the streets. Here they gathered any hour of the day or night to discuss in muffled tones the latest scrap of gossip. The game wardens had found several carcasses already in the brush just south of town. Someone had seen a buck and a doe on the Winton road not over a mile away. As the time drew close, men who hitherto had worn the calm placid look of substantial citizens, now had the preoccupied expressions of those about to embark upon great and desperate adventure.

Those last few days were interminable, then all of a sudden the hour was upon us. Final hurried preparations and checking over of supplies, all but tearful goodbyes from our wives. "There had been so many accidents already. We would be careful, wouldn't we? Good luck and have a good time," fell upon heedless ears and we were off.

As we roared out of town, the tension snapped and we were our old selves again. If we had cared to

confess it however, there had been a lot of satisfaction in the fuss we had caused at that and in the incidental adulation that followed us out. My own little Junior had followed me around admiringly for a whole week, weighing my every word. But today when I donned my wool stag pants, checkered shirt and suspenders, his joy was unconcealed. To him I was as completely Sir Galahad as though I had worn a suit of shining armor. I had promised him faithfully a very rash promise, made I'll admit in a mood of braggadocio, to bring home the biggest buck in the woods, with horns a yard wide and full fashioned. For that matter, we were heroes to every youngster in town if not to our wives. It was satisfying to know that once again we could bask in the role of the primitive provider, faring forth to deeds of "derring do."

We were bound for the Stony River country, the choicest bit of hunting ground in northern Minnesota. Since the days of the lumberjacks, the word "Stony" has been one of more than ordinary meaning wherever the subject of deer hunting has come up. Just mention that name to any nimrod in the northern half of the state and see his eyes light up. Ten chances to one, he will start the inevitable "I remember" and then you'll be in for an all night session.

Thirty miles of driving over the crookedest road in creation brought us through the heart of the "Superior National Forest" to the banks of the Stony River. Here we left our car in the clearing of what used to be old camp six in the logging days, and struck due east into the brush. After following the north bank for several miles, we pitched camp just as it was getting dark in a heavy growth of mixed timber near the water.

After an hour or two of the usual milling around that accompanies the setting up of camp, we settled down to enjoy ourselves and make ready with the necessary word barrage for the morning's attack.

The fire of pine knots was burning merrily, throwing a ghostly light on the tall white trunks of birch and aspen. The dean looked at his watch. "Ten hours and twenty minutes to go," he announced. "Within half a day, we'll hear the crack of rifles."

We gave our guns a final polishing, while we planned the morning's hunt. Glenn would go up the narrows, the dean west along the river, Hilliard and

*A curious yet wary buck looks for signs of intruders into his domain. (Photo © Len Rue, Jr.)*

I would work north toward Dunnigan Lake. One thing worried us more than anything else and that was the absence of snow. Deer hunting with the leaves dry and noisy and no possible chance of tracking was a condition to be dreaded. Yet here we were confronted by the very thing we had hoped and prayed wouldn't happen.

"I remember the season of '21," spoke Glenn. "The woods were so confoundedly noisy then that you couldn't get within a mile of anything. Didn't have a ghost of a chance."

"You're certainly a cheerful cuss," I answered. "Seems to me we had good shooting that year, although I will admit we had to work for what we got."

"The only way tomorrow," concluded Hilliard after an hour of reminiscing, "is to pick a spot and sit down. There's no earthly use in moving around."

"Guess you're right," agreed the dean. "Let 'em come to you. There's no use chasing 'em tomorrow."

I got up and walked out of the circle of firelight to take a look at the sky. It was cloudy and the wind was in the south. A slight chance but doubtful. Nine o'clock found us in our sleeping bags. The last long night was under way.

Long before daylight, I heard a whisper, "Pile out you swamp angels, it's almost time." It was the dean, as I might have guessed. He never could sleep worth a damn the night before. I looked at my watch. It was only four-thirty and wouldn't be light for another two hours.

"Start the fire," I mumbled, "and when it's nice and warm, call me." A disgusted snort was my only answer.

In a moment a candle sputtered into a sickly yellow flame. By this time, Glenn too was awake. "What's the idea," he roared. "This ain't duck season. Poor devil, he's gone completely off—." A flying boot hushed him up.

It wasn't long before a fire was blazing in front of the tent, throwing a warm and pleasant glow against the side of my sleeping bag. Never in all my life had I been so thoroughly comfortable. The fringe of trees outside the circle of firelight looked dark and mysterious. Somewhere back in the gloom, a branch snapped. It was a dark and forbidding world and I snuggled farther down in my bag. The smell of boil-

*A large buck stands silhouetted against the sunlight filtered through the leaves. (Photo © Leonard Lee Rue III)*

Above: *A buck mates with a doe in the middle of a raspberry patch.* (Photo © Bruce Montagne)
Facing page: *A whitetail buck lip-curls to test a female's urine during the rut.* (Photo © Len Rue, Jr.)

ing coffee was tempting and so was the bacon.

"Come on you birds," growled the dean in desperation, "what sort of a tea party do you think this is?"

His sarcasm had the desired effect. "Here goes nothing," came from Hilliard, as he burst from his bag. I followed suit and so did Glenn. For the next few minutes, the tent was a nightmare of woolen underwear, stag pants and suspenders. Coffee over and cigarettes and still it wasn't daylight. We busied ourselves stowing away chocolate bars, sandwiches, shells and advice. The dean was pulling on his cap and without as much as a parting word, he lifted the flap and was gone. We were on our way.

There was not a breath of air and the woods so quiet it hurt to move. My first step in the dry crackly leaves all but unnerved me. After going a short distance, I stopped to listen. The others were gradually crunching off into the brush, Hilliard and Glenn to my right, the dean to my left. A partridge whirred up in front of me and lit in the top of a birch where he proceeded to make his breakfast on the frozen brown buds. From the timber in back came the rolling tattoo of a downy woodpecker drilling away at a dead pine stub.

I had gone perhaps a quarter of a mile, when I heard a different sound, the rapid pattering of running hoofs on a hard dry trail. I stopped again to listen, there was no mistake. The dean had jumped a couple and they were coming my way. Crouching, I ran swiftly forward toward a trail on the next ridge. The brush was so thick I couldn't see more than a few feet in front of me. When I reached the ridge, I climbed a stump and waited. The pattering sound had stopped. Had they gone or were they watching me? I stood it a moment longer and then stepped down. There was a snort and a crash and the deer burst from their cover in a thicket of alder and bounded away down the trail. As luck would have it, I didn't see a flash. Two seconds sooner and I'd have had shooting. I stood and listened until I could no longer hear them moving and then walked down the trail to where they had stood. It was as I had thought, a buck and a doe.

All photos: *The strides of a whitetail buck running for safety. (Photos © Leonard Lee Rue III)*

Picking out a likely looking spot, I sat down to wait. Perhaps the dean would scare up another. In a way I was glad I had missed my first chance. It would have been a shame to have made my kill so early. An hour passed without a sound but the nervous rustling of dry leaves.

Just as I rose to go, bang-bang-bang sounded far to my right toward the narrows. That must be Glenn. A little later came another shot, the "Coup de Grace." First blood of the season.

I wandered around the edge of a swamp grown thickly with black spruce and alder, and paused on top of a high ridge. Suddenly the brush cracked sharply down below me. All tense, I waited. Crash again, something was surely coming. Moving to a better vantage point, I slipped the safety off and got set. The whole valley was in plain view before me. Then out of the corner of my eye, I caught a telltale flash of red, brilliant eye-splitting red. I lowered my gun in disgust, not that I wouldn't have liked to shoot, but all that suspense for nothing.

I sat down carefully so as not to attract attention. On he came, someone else's Sir Galahad, running like a fool. Not once did he look my way and for that I was glad. In a short time he disappeared and I vaguely regretted the fact that he had proceeded in the direction my deer had taken.

Cutting across his trail, I started off at right angles to his course through the swamp. Five minutes later, I was startled by a series of rapid shots. My friend of the brilliant topknot had connected. After that, firing broke out in all directions. First came a volley from Deep Lake toward the east, then from old camp six, and last from the Dunnigan Lake country ahead of me. Everyone seemed to be getting shooting but me. It was disquieting to say the least, particularly when reflecting that I had hunted deer for almost twenty years, had guided scores of parties myself, and was generally considered an old hand at the game. Above all, I had my reputation with Junior to uphold. He could not be disappointed—the biggest buck in the woods—horns a yard wide and full fashioned.

I tightened up my belt and settled down to hunt in earnest. No more time for scenery or reflection. The leaves were so confoundedly noisy and though I took advantage of every moss covered rock and log, my progress must have been broadcasted for a mile.

The racket I made was terrible. Today it was a case of pure luck.

Noon found me on a bare pine-covered ridge far to the northward. Here was a wonderful chance to watch. The sun came out and with it the shooting increased. The deer were moving around again. While I ate my lunch, I watched the country below me. Open rolling ridges extended in three directions and I could see for hundreds of yards. After all, the hunting wasn't everything and there were other days coming.

It was pleasant sitting there in the sun even though I knew that I ought to be moving around. A squirrel scrambled up the jackpine to my right and heaped upon my poor defenseless head all the vile squirrelish blasphemy he could think of. Then as if satisfied that anything as big and stupid as I was could certainly be of no importance, he scurried down the way he had come and continued his belated harvesting. A little later, a pair of soft grey whiskey jacks dropped in from nowhere and gave me the once over.

I don't know how long I sat there, but it was probably much longer than I should have. Leaving the hilltop almost regretfully, I turned south and headed toward camp. It was now the middle of the afternoon and by four-thirty it would be too dark to shoot. I would have to hurry.

Half a mile further on, I came to a beaver pond. This was good country, lots of swamp grass, willow and other feed around the edges. A beaver dam at the lower end of the pond served as a bridge. I made it across safely and strolled up a well marked trail on the other side. Everywhere were signs, places they had pawed the ground for roots and rubbing trees the bucks had used to polish the velvet off their horns. Here I would have to watch myself. As quietly as I could, I worked my way up the slope.

When I reached the top, I stopped to look the country over. Suddenly there was a racket in the swamp below me. A ridge a hundred yards away would command the trail. There was only one thing to do, make a spurt for it. I made it in ten flat, of that I'm certain. Throwing myself down in true skirmish fashion, I waited. Something moved through the brush to my left. That was all, not a flash did I see, but I heard my deer crashing through the thin ice of the muskeg below. If I had only been two seconds sooner; another of the possibilities that pepper every hunting season.

A little later, while working through a brushy ravine, I stopped to take a look at my compass. While slipping off my glove, there was a crash ahead of me. For a frantic instant, I struggled to free my hand, while the white flag of a deer bounced gaily through the timber. One parting snap shot was all I got.

By now, I was fully convinced that I was the original "faux pas." Although I had just passed through a long season of duck shooting, where I had relearned for the ten thousandth time the old lesson not to be caught napping, here I was blundering around as though I had never had a gun in my hands.

It was dark before I reached the river. The fire showed up a long ways off, gleaming a steady red beacon through the trees. The others were in ahead of me and as I approached, I could see their red top knots shining in the firelight. There was no meat in camp as yet, at least none that I could see. Perhaps, I hadn't been so unfortunate after all.

Glenn was the first to look up. "Well," he remarked, "where's that heart and liver. We've got the frying pan all greased up and hot waiting for it."

That gave me my clue, or so I thought. Leaning my rifle against a tree, I took the place reserved for me in the circle, lit a cigarette and answered as casually as possible, "speaking of heart and liver, I guess mine is doing duty like the rest."

At that there was a raising of eyebrows and an exchange of glances that could only be interpreted in one way. Someone had killed a deer.

"Get any shooting at all?" asked the dean, after a weighty moment's silence.

"Nothing but a snap shot," I answered. "Couldn't get within a mile of anything today." Then remembering the shooting I had heard toward the narrows early in the morning, I turned around to Glenn and asked him to come across.

Without a word, he rose, walked over to a tree behind the tent and lifted something from a crotch. Then coming over to me, he held it under my nose for inspection. It was a heart and liver, sure enough.

Without any further urging, he told how a spike buck had all but walked over him on the trail alongside the narrows. Then as though that wasn't enough, Hilliard piped up and told how he too had dropped a nice little doe near Dunnigan Lake. The dean was still in my class and I could see that the

*Caught in midair, a whitetail buck glides as it runs. (Photo © Denver Bryan)*

situation rankled, for he too was supposed to be experienced.

That evening we spent praying for snow and cold, snow for tracking and cold to freeze the river solid enough so that we could snake our deer out on the ice. The prospect of a four mile carry through the woods was anything but pleasant. If it stayed warm, it might even necessitate cutting up our meat and packing it in quarters and that was a possibility that none of us relished. We all felt the same way about it. The wallop was half gone if we couldn't bring our deer in whole and then for me, there was my promise to Junior.

"We're never satisfied," spoke Hilliard at last. "During duck season, it's rain and cold, when we're fishing, it's got to be cloudy, and now snow. You'd think that the only time it's possible for us to have any luck, is when it's miserable."

"It's all right for you to talk," grumbled the dean, "your reputation is safe."

Next morning, bright and early, we hit the trail. There were only two of us hunting, Glenn and Hilliard having planned to spend the day dragging theirs in to camp.

I hunted in the same general direction I had taken the day before. Mid-afternoon found me on a heavily timbered ridge overlooking a frozen grassy swale below. Here was as wild and likely a looking spot as I had ever seen, and strangely enough, I had the premonition that here I would make my kill. Not having kept track of my direction since leaving camp, it seemed as though I was miles away. I remember distinctly, wondering at the time, as though the kill were already a settled fact, how in the world I would ever get my meat out.

I settled down then to wait at a spot where I could overlook all but one small corner of the swale, hidden by a heavy clump of young jack pine half ways down the slope. I thought some of moving to the top of the ridge from where I knew I would have a clear view, but dismissed it as an unnecessary precaution. Besides, I was very comfortable where I was.

Ten minutes passed, then down across the swamp, a branch cracked sharply. I looked up. A brown form moved slowly through the alder brush bordering the opening and then disappeared. I waited expectantly. Presently, a big buck stalked boldly out and started crossing the swamp. Now I had occasion to curse, for the clump of jack pine was directly in line. Although I could see him plainly through the dense screen of branches, it was impossible to shoot. Why hadn't I followed my first hunch and moved? I sat there helplessly and watched him work his way to the center of the pothole. There he stopped and proceeded to paw through the thin ice for water. I could have tried a shot then, but decided to wait. Perhaps he would keep on coming toward me and cross the ridge I was on.

He drank daintily and started on once more. I could see now that he had a wonderful spread of horns. Never in all my life will I forget that moment. On he came, as though he had all the time in the world, as yet oblivious of the death that awaited him on the other side.

So far, I hadn't had a decent shot, though several times I saw him fairly well through the screen of branches before me. Once I thought of shooting, but he disappeared while I was getting my bead. He was now at the base of my ridge, well hidden in a dense growth of alder. I could hear him plainly, moving around, feeding on the brush. Now was my chance. Leaving my hiding place, I crawled swiftly to the top of the ridge where I should have been in the first place. There wasn't a sound from the thicket now and for a moment I was overwhelmed with the sickening thought that he was gone. Perhaps, he was standing still, listening and getting the wind.

It wasn't long before I heard him again, now coming directly toward me. Once I saw a movement in the brush, but it was gone in an instant. The buck was now within a hundred feet of me, but still I couldn't see him. If he should come out, it would be nothing but sheer murder and I instinctively recoiled at the thought of making a kill at that range.

Suddenly I saw a movement behind a bunch of balsams not seventy-five feet away; just a swaying of the branches, nothing more. Then he stopped dead and for the first time, I know he was suspicious. Now things began to happen. With a wild snort, the deer wheeled, crashed down the slope and to my joy headed for the swamp the way he had come. He hit the grass going like the wind, flag up and horns back, twenty feet at a jump. I drew a hurried bead on his shoulder and fired. It was a clean miss. Another bead

*A beautiful buck with wide, low-spread antlers. (Photo © Len Rue, Jr.)*

Above: *A whitetail buck rubs his antlers over the trunk of a sapling during the rut. (Photo © Leonard Lee Rue III)*
Facing page: *A whitetail buck on the edge of a Florida cypress swamp. (Photo © Erwin and Peggy Bauer)*

at the point of his nose and he dropped almost out of sight in the muskeg.

I waited a moment to see if he would get up and then ran down to where he lay. He was stone dead and queerly enough did not have a bullet mark on him. Not until I had him cleaned did a telltale drop of blood give the secret away. I had hit him at the base of the skull, the bullet having penetrated between the ears without even ruffling the hair.

I sat down upon a hummock of moss after I was all through and took a long deferred smoke. My buck was a nice one, about two hundred pounds in weight and with good horns, full fashioned too. I rested for half an hour and lived through once more every second of the time I'd spent on the jack pine ridge above me. By now the whiskey jacks had begun to gather and I was ready to move.

Throwing some brush over the carcass, I left, blazing a north-south line toward the river. To my surprise, it was only a little over a mile. My

zigzagging had fooled me, but at that it was far enough.

No one was in camp, but a nice spike buck and a doe were hanging alongside the tent. Glenn and Hilliard had gotten theirs in. They must have gone out again to help bring in the dean's. Some time later, as I was enjoying a cup of coffee, I heard a yell from the direction of the river. I got up and ran down to the shore. It was the dean dragging his along the ice. Glenn and Hilliard came in shortly afterwards. They had struck the ice a mile above camp and the dean against their advice, had proceeded to take his deer down the river in spite of the fact that it had been thawing all day. Now we all went down to help and to the tune of cracking ice dragged the doe ashore and up to camp.

That night, we recounted our many adventures over and over again, elaborating and polishing, until each tale had become a finished product that could bear telling and retelling without the danger of plagiarism. It was a night to be remembered. For once we were at peace with the world

The next few days might better be gone over briefly. Much to our disgust, the weather turned warmer, making the swamps impassable and worst of all weakening the ice hopelessly on the river. Although we hated to admit it, we were up against it as far as getting our game out whole was concerned. We waited but in vain. The sun kept on shining and the wind stayed in the south. There was only one thing left to do, quarter our animals and pack them in as so much duffle. It was a disheartening joy to say the least, to bid goodbye to all hopes of a grand triumphant entry.

As we drove into town that last night my courage all but left me. Junior met me at the gate as I knew he would.

A wild yell of greeting and then, "Daddy, where's your deer?"

I pointed at the pack sack tied to the running board. He took one look and his jaw dropped. "Daddy, I thought—" and he buried his disappointment in the rough folds of my mackinaw. One Stag Pants Galahad had fallen from grace.

Left: *A whitetail doe dashes through the snow. (Photo © D. Robert Franz)*
Overleaf: *Whitetail country: The moon overlooks a hazy Florida prairie. (Photo © Chica Stracener)*

# RACE AT MORNING

## by William Faulkner

William Faulkner had Mississippi in his bones. He lived most of his life in the town of Oxford in the hill country above the famous Mississippi Delta, just south of Memphis. He hunted the woods, bayous, and thickets, and he also wrote his series of novels and short stories that eventually won him the 1949 Nobel Prize for Literature. Those writings told of Faulkner's mythical Yoknapatawpha County, its landscape and denizens, and included his grand novels of the South, such as *The Sound and the Fury, Light in August, As I Lay Dying*, and *Absalom, Absalom!* In addition to the Nobel Prize, he won the Pulitzer Prize twice: in 1955, for *A Fable*, and in 1963, for his final, picaresque novel, *The Reivers*.

Faulkner's writing is rich in the lore and language of Mississippi, and thus it should be no surprise that he also wrote of hunting with a passion. Many of his novels include scenes of hunts that are stunning in their description, evoking the sweat, scents, and sounds of a Mississippi hunt. Faulkner's 1955 collection of hunting short stories, *Big Woods*, includes this tale of a young boy and a wise old man in a race for a big buck, a buck that haunts their land—and their imaginations.

I was in the boat when I seen him. It was jest dust-dark; I had jest fed the horses and clumb back down the bank to the boat and shoved off to cross back to camp when I seen him, about half a quarter up the river, swimming; jest his head above the water, and it no more than a dot in that light. But I could see that rocking chair he toted on it and I knowed it was him, going right back to that canebrake in the fork of the bayou where he lived all year until the day before the season opened, like the game wardens had give him a calendar, when he would clear out and disappear, nobody knowed where, until the day after the season closed. But here he was, coming back a day ahead of time, like maybe he had got mixed up and was using last year's calendar by mistake. Which was jest too bad for him, because me and Mister Ernest would be setting on the horse right over him when the sun rose tomorrow morning.

So I told Mister Ernest and we et supper and fed the dogs, and then I holp Mister Ernest in the poker game, standing behind his chair until about ten o'clock, when Roth Edmonds said, "Why don't you go to bed, boy?"

*A majestic whitetail buck outlined by the orange hues of sunrise. (Photo © T. Urban)*

"Or if you're going to set up," Willy Legate said, "why don't you take a spelling book to set up over? He knows every cuss word in the dictionary, every poker hand in the deck and every whisky label in the distillery, but he can't even write his name. Can you?" he says to me.

"I don't need to write my name down," I said. "I can remember in my mind who I am."

"You're twelve years old," Walter Ewell said. "Man to man now, how many days in your life did you ever spend in school?"

"He ain't got time to go to school," Willy Legate said. "What's the use in going to school from September to middle of November, when he'll have to quit then to come in here and do Ernest's hearing for him? And what's the use in going back to school in January, when in jest eleven months it will be November fifteenth again and he'll have to start all over telling Ernest which way the dogs went?"

"Well, stop looking into my hand, anyway," Roth Edmonds said.

"What's that? What's that?" Mister Ernest said. He wore his listening button in his ear all the time, but he never brought the battery to camp with him because the cord would bound to get snagged ever time we run through a thicket.

"Willy says for me to go to bed!" I hollered.

"Don't you never call nobody 'mister'?" Willy said.

"I call Mister Ernest 'mister,'" I said.

"All right," Mister Ernest said. "Go to bed then. I don't need you."

"That ain't no lie," Willy said. "Deaf or no deaf, he can hear a fifty-dollar raise if you don't even move your lips."

So I went to bed, and after a while Mister Ernest come in and I wanted to tell him again how big them horns looked even half a quarter away in the river. Only I would 'a' had to holler, and the only time Mister Ernest agreed he couldn't hear was when we would be setting on Dan, waiting for me to point which way the dogs was going. So we jest laid down, and it wasn't no time Simon was beating the bottom of the dishpan with the spoon, hollering, "Raise up and get your four-o'clock coffee!" and I crossed the river in the dark this time, with the lantern, and fed Dan and Roth Edmondziz horse. It was going to be a fine day, cold and bright; even in the dark I could see the white frost on the leaves and bushes—jest exactly the kind of day that big old son of a gun laying up there in that brake would like to run.

Then we et, and set the stand-holder across for Uncle Ike McCaslin to put them on the stands where he thought they ought to be, because he was the oldest one in camp. He had been hunting deer in these woods for about a hundred years, I reckon, and if anybody would know where a buck would pass, it would be him. Maybe with a big old buck like this one, that had been running the woods for what would amount to a hundred years in a deer's life, too, him and Uncle Ike would sholy manage to be at the same place at the same time this morning—provided, of course, he managed to git away from me and Mister Ernest on the jump. Because me and Mister Ernest was going to git him.

Then me and Mister Ernest and Roth Edmonds sent the dogs over, with Simon holding Eagle and the other old dogs on leash because the young ones, the puppies, wasn't going nowhere until Eagle let them, nohow. Then me and Mister Ernest and Roth saddled up, and Mister Ernest got up and I handed him up his pump gun and let Dan's bridle go for him to git rid of the spell of bucking he had to git shut of ever morning until Mister Ernest hit him between the ears with the gun barrel. Then Mister Ernest loaded the gun and give me the stirrup, and I got up behind him and we taken the fire road up toward the bayou, the four big dogs dragging Simon along in front with his singlebarrel britchloader slung on a piece of plow line across his back, and the puppies moiling along in ever'body's way. It was light now and it was going to be jest fine; the east already yellow for the sun and our breaths smoking in the cold still bright air until the sun would come up and warm it, and a little skim of ice in the ruts, and ever leaf and twig and switch and even the frozen clods frosted over, waiting to sparkle like a rainbow when the sun finally come up and hit them. Until all my insides felt light and strong as a balloon, full of that light cold strong air, so that it seemed to me like I couldn't even feel the horse's back I was straddle of—jest the hot strong muscles moving under the hot strong skin, setting up there without no weight atall, so that when old Eagle struck and jumped, me and Dan and Mister Ernest would go jest like a bird, not even touching the ground. It was jest fine. When that

*A large buck runs full-out over the snow in pursuit of a whitetail doe. (Photo © Bill Marchel)*

big old buck got killed today, I knowed that even if he had put it off another ten years, he couldn't 'a' picked a better one.

And sho enough, as soon as we come to the bayou we seen his foot in the mud where he had come up out of the river last night, spread in the soft mud like a cow's foot, big as a cow's, big as a mule's, with Eagle and the other dogs laying into the leash rope now until Mister Ernest told me to jump down and help Simon hold them. Because me and Mister Ernest knowed exactly where he would be—a little canebrake island in the middle of the bayou, where he could lay up until whatever doe or little deer the dogs had happened to jump could go up or down

the bayou in either direction and take the dogs on away, so he could steal out and creep back down the bayou to the river and swim it, and leave the country like he always done the day the season opened.

Which is jest what we never aimed for him to do this time. So we left Roth on his horse to cut him off and turn him over Uncle Ike's standers if he tried to slip back down the bayou, and me and Simon, with the leashed dogs, walked on up the bayou until Mister Ernest on the horse said it was fur enough; then turned up into the woods about half a quarter above the brake because the wind was going to be south this morning when it riz, and turned down toward the brake, and Mister Ernest give the word to cast

them, and we slipped the leash and Mister Ernest give me the stirrup again and I got up.

Old Eagle had done already took off because he knowed where that old son of a gun would be laying as good as we did, not making no racket atall yet, but jest boring on through the buck vines with the other dogs trailing along behind him, and even Dan seemed to know about that buck, too, beginning to souple up and jump a little through the vines, so that I taken my holt on Mister Ernest's belt already before the time had come for Mister Ernest to touch him. Because when we got strung out, going fast behind a deer, I wasn't on Dan's back much of the time nohow, but mostly jest strung out from my holt on Mister Ernest's belt, so that Willy Legate said that when we was going through the woods fast, it looked like Mister Ernest had a boy-size pair of empty overalls blowing out of his hind pocket.

So it wasn't even a strike, it was a jump. Eagle must 'a' walked right up behind him or maybe even stepped on him while he was laying there still thinking it was day after tomorrow. Eagle jest throwed his head back and up and said, "There he goes," and we even heard the buck crashing through the first of the cane. Then all the other dogs was hollering behind him, and Dan give a squat to jump, but it was against the curb this time, not jest the snaffle, and Mister Ernest let him down into the bayou and swung him around the brake and up the other bank. Only he never had to say, "Which way?" because I was already pointing past his shoulder, freshening my holt on the belt jest as Mister Ernest touched Dan with that big old rusty spur on his nigh heel, because when Dan felt it he would go off jest like a stick of dynamite, straight through whatever he could bust and over or under what he couldn't, over it like a bird or under it crawling on his knees like a mole or a big coon, with Mister Ernest still on him because he had the saddle to hold on to, and me still there because I had Mister Ernest to hold on to; me and Mister Ernest not riding him, but jest going along with him, provided we held on. Because when the jump come, Dan never cared who else was there neither; I believe to my soul he could 'a' cast and run them dogs by hisself, without me or Mister Ernest or Simon or nobody.

That's what he done. He had to; the dogs was already almost out of hearing. Eagle must 'a' been looking right up that big son of a gun's tail until he finally decided he better git on out of there. And now they must 'a' been getting pretty close to Uncle Ike's standers, and Mister Ernest reined Dan back and held him, squatting and bouncing and trembling like a mule having his tail roached, while we listened for the shots. But never none come, and I hollered to Mister Ernest we better go on while I could still hear the dogs, and he let Dan off, but still there wasn't no shots, and now we knowed the race had done already passed the standers, like that old son of a gun actually was a hant, like Simon and the other field hands said he was, and we busted out of a thicket, and sho enough there was Uncle Ike and Willy standing beside his foot in a soft patch.

"He got through us all," Uncle Ike said. "I don't know how he done it. I just had a glimpse of him. He looked big as a elephant, with a rack on his head you could cradle a yellin' calf in. He went right on down the ridge. You better get on, too; that Hog Bayou camp might not miss him."

So I freshened my holt and Mister Ernest touched Dan again. The ridge run due south; it was clear of vines and bushes so we could go fast, into the wind, too, because it had riz now, and now the sun was up, too; though I hadn't had time to notice it, bright and strong and level through the woods, shining and sparking like a rainbow on the frosted leaves. So we would hear the dogs again any time now as the wind got up; we could make time now, but still holding Dan back to a canter, because it was either going to be quick, when he got down to the standers from that Hog Bayou camp eight miles below ourn, or a long time, in case he got by them, too. And sho enough, after a while we heard the dogs; we was walking Dan now to let him blow a while, and we heard them, the sound coming faint up the wind, not running now, but trailing because the big son of a gun had decided a good piece back, probably, to put a end to this foolishness, and picked hisself up and souled out and put about a mile between hisself and the dogs—until he run up on them other standers from that camp below. I could almost see him stopped behind a bush, peeping out and saying, "What's this? What's this? Is this whole durn country full of folks this morning?" Then looking

*Elusive at any time, a whitetail buck is nearly concealed by a morning fog. (Photo © D. Robert Franz)*

back over his shoulder at where old Eagle and the others was hollering along after him while he decided how much time he had to decide what to do next.

Except he almost shaved it too fine. We heard the shots; it sounded like a war. Old Eagle must 'a' been looking right up his tail again and he had to bust on through the best way he could. "Pow, pow, pow, pow" and then "Pow, pow, pow, pow," like it must 'a' been three or four ganged right up on him before he had time even to swerve, and me hollering, "No! No! No! No!" because he was ourn. It was our beans and oats he et and our brake he laid in; we had been watching him every year, and it was like we had raised him, to be killed at last on our jump, in front of our dogs, by some strangers that would probably try to beat the dogs off and drag him away before we could even git a piece of the meat.

"Shut up and listen," Mister Ernest said. So I done it and we could hear the dogs; not just the others, but Eagle, too, not trailing no scent now and not baying no downed meat neither, but running hot on sight long after the shooting was over. I jest had time to freshen my holt. Yes, sir, they was running on sight. Like Willy Legate would say, if Eagle jest had a drink of whisky he would ketch that deer; going on, done already gone when we broke out of the thicket and seen the fellers that had done the shooting, five or six of them, squatting and crawling around, looking at the ground and the bushes, like maybe if they looked hard enough, spots of blood would bloom out on the stalks and leaves like frogstools or hawberries, with old Eagle still in hearing and still telling them that what blood they found wasn't coming out of nothing in front of him.

"Have any luck, boys?" Mister Ernest said.

"I think I hit him," one of them said. "I know I did. We're hunting blood now."

"Well, when you find him, blow your horn and I'll come back and tote him in to camp for you," Mister Ernest said.

So we went on, going fast now because the race was almost out of hearing again, going fast, too, like not jest the buck, but the dogs, too, had took a new leash on life from all the excitement and shooting.

We was in strange country now because we never had to run this fur before, we had always killed be-

*With a grace belying its bulk, a whitetail buck leaps over a barbed-wire fence. (Photo © Stephen Kirkpatrick)*

fore now; now we had come to Hog Bayou that runs into the river a good fifteen miles below our camp. It had water in it, not to mention a mess of down trees and logs and such, and Mister Ernest checked Dan again, saying, "Which way?" I could just barely hear them, off to the east a little, like the old son of a gun had give up the idea of Vicksburg or New Orleans, like he first seemed to have, and had decided to have a look at Alabama, maybe, since he was already up and moving; so I pointed and we turned up the bayou hunting for a crossing, and maybe we could 'a' found one, except that I reckon Mister Ernest decided we never had time to wait.

We come to a place where the bayou had narrowed down to about twelve or fifteen feet, and Mister Ernest said, "Look out, I'm going to touch him" and done it; I didn't even have time to freshen my holt when we was already in the air, and then I seen the vine—it was a loop of grapevine nigh as big as my wrist, looping down right across the middle of the bayou—and I thought he seen it, too, and was jest waiting to grab it and fling it up over our heads to go under it, and I know Dan seen it because he even ducked his head to jump under it. But Mister Ernest never seen it atall until it skun back along Dan's neck and hooked under the head of the saddle horn, us flying on through the air, the loop of the vine gitting tighter and tighter until something somewhere was going to have to give. It was the saddle girth. It broke, and Dan going on and scrabbling up the other bank bare nekkid except for the bridle, and me and Mister Ernest and the saddle, Mister Ernest still setting in the saddle holding the gun, and me still holding onto Mister Ernest's belt, hanging in the air over the bayou in the tightened loop of that vine like in the drawed-back loop of a big rubber-banded slingshot, until it snapped back and shot us back across the bayou and flang us clear, me still holding onto Mister Ernest's belt and on the bottom now, so that when we lit I would 'a' had Mister Ernest and the saddle both on top of me if I hadn't clumb fast around the saddle and up Mister Ernest's side, so that when we landed, it was the saddle first, then Mister Ernest, and me on top, until I jumped up, and Mister Ernest still laying there with jest the white rim of his eyes showing.

"Mister Ernest!" I hollered, and then clumb down to the bayou and scooped my cap full of water and clumb back and threwed it in his face, and he opened his eyes and laid there on the saddle cussing me.

"God dawg it," he said, "why didn't you stay behind where you started out?"

"You was the biggest!" I said. "You would 'a' mashed me flat!"

"What do you think you done to me?" Mister Ernest said. "Next time, if you can't stay where you start out, jump clear. Don't climb up on top of me no more. You hear?"

"Yes, sir," I said.

So he got up then, still cussing and holding his back, and clumb down to the water and dipped some in his hand onto his face and neck and dipped some more up and drunk it, and I drunk some, too, and clumb back and got the saddle and the gun, and we crossed the bayou on the down logs. If we could jest ketch Dan; not that he would have went them fifteen miles back to camp, because, if anything, he would have went on by hisself to try to help Eagle ketch that buck. But he was about fifty yards away, eating buck vines, so I brought him back, and we taken Mister Ernest's galluses and my belt and the whang leather loop off Mister Ernest's horn and tied the saddle back on Dan. It didn't look like much, but maybe it would hold.

"Provided you don't let me jump him through no more grapevines without hollering first," Mister Ernest said.

"Yes, sir," I said. "I'll holler first next time—provided you'll holler a little quicker when you touch him next time, too." But it was all right; we jest had to be a little easy getting up. "Now which-a-way?" I said. Because we couldn't hear nothing now, after wasting all this time. And this was new country, sho enough. It had been cut over and growed up in thickets we couldn't 'a' seen over even standing up on Dan.

But Mister Ernest never even answered. He jest turned Dan along the bank of the bayou where it was a little more open and we could move faster again, soon as Dan and us got used to that homemade cinch strop and got a little confidence in it. Which jest happened to be east, or so I thought then, because I never paid no particular attention to east then because the sun—I don't know where the morn-

*With its majestic rack of antlers held high, a whitetail buck commands a view of the Texas brush. (Photo © Steve Bentsen)*

ing had went, but it was gone, the morning and the frost, too—was up high now, even if my insides had told me it was past dinnertime.

And then we heard him. No, that's wrong; what we heard was shots. And that was when we realized how fur we had come, because the only camp we knowed about in that direction was the Hollyknowe camp, and Hollyknowe was exactly twenty-eight miles from Van Dorn, where me and Mister Ernest lived—jest the shots, no dogs nor nothing. If old Eagle was still behind him and the buck was still alive, he was too wore out now to even say, "Here he comes."

"Don't touch him!" I hollered. But Mister Ernest remembered that cinch strop, too, and he jest let Dan off the snaffle. And Dan heard them shots, too, picking his way through the thickets, hopping the vines and logs when he could and going under them when he couldn't. And sho enough, it was jest like before—two or three men squatting and creeping among the bushes, looking for blood that Eagle had done already told them wasn't there. But we never stopped this time, jest trotting on by with Dan hopping and dodging among the brush and vines dainty as a dancer. Then Mister Ernest swung Dan until we was going due north.

"Wait!" I hollered. "Not this way."

But Mister Ernest jest turned his face back over his shoulder. It looked tired, too, and there was a smear of mud on it where that ere grapevine had snatched him off the horse.

"Don't you know where he's heading?" he said. "He's done done his part, give everybody a fair open shot at him, and now he's going home, back to that brake in our bayou. He ought to make it exactly at dark."

And that's what he was doing. We went on. It didn't matter to hurry now. There wasn't no sound nowhere; it was that time in the early afternoon in November when don't nothing move or cry, not even birds, the peckerwoods and yellowhammers and jays, and it seemed to me like I could see all three of us— me and Mister Ernest and Dan— and Eagle, and the other dogs, and that big old buck, moving through the quiet woods in the same direction, headed for the same place, not running now but walking, that had all run the fine race the best we knowed how,

and all three of us now turned like on a agreement to walk back home, not together in a bunch because we didn't want to worry or tempt one another, because what we had all three spent this morning doing was no play-acting jest for fun, but was serious, and all three of us was still what we was—that old buck that had to run, not because he was skeered, but because running was what he done the best and was proudest at; and Eagle and the dogs that chased him, not because they hated or feared him, but because that was the thing they done the best and was proudest at; and me and Mister Ernest and Dan, that run him not because we wanted his meat, which would be too tough to eat anyhow, or his head to hang on a wall, but because now we could go back and work hard for eleven months making a crop, so we would have the right to come back here next November—all three of us going back home now, peaceful and separate, but still side by side, until next year, next time.

Then we seen him for the first time. We was out of the cut-over now; we could even 'a' cantered, except that all three of us was long past that, and now you could tell where west was because the sun was already halfway down it. So we was walking, too, when we come on the dogs—the puppies and one of the old ones—played out, laying in a little wet swag, panting, jest looking up at us when we passed, but not moving when we went on. Then we come to a long open glade, you could see about half a quarter, and we seen the three other old dogs and about a hundred yards ahead of them Eagle, all walking, not making no sound; and then suddenly, at the fur end of the glade, the buck hisself getting up from where he had been resting for the dogs to come up, getting up without no hurry, big, big as a mule, tall as a mule, and turned without no hurry still, and the white underside of his tail for a second or two more before the thicket taken him.

It might 'a' been a signal, a good-bye, a farewell. Still walking, we passed the other three old dogs in the middle of the glade, laying down, too, now jest where they was when the buck vanished, and not trying to get up neither when we passed; and still that hundred yards ahead of them, Eagle, too, not laying down, because he was still on his feet, but his legs

Facing page: *A whitetail doe drinks, her image reflected across the surface of the pond. (Photo © Michael H. Francis)*
Overleaf: *A Florida buck lip-curls during the rut to determine if nearby does are ready to mate. (Photo © Chica Stracener)*

was spraddled and his head was down; maybe jest waiting until we was out of sight of his shame, his eyes saying plain as talk when we passed, "I'm sorry, boys, but this here is all."

Mister Ernest stopped Dan. "Jump down and look at his feet," he said.

"Ain't nothing wrong with his feet," I said. "It's his wind has done give out."

"Jump down and look at his feet," Mister Ernest said.

So I done it, and while I was stooping over Eagle I could hear the pump gun go, "Snick-cluck. Snick-cluck. Snick-cluck" three times, except that I never thought nothing then. Maybe he was jest running the shells through to be sho it would work when we seen him again or maybe to make sho they was all buckshot. Then I got up again, and we went on, still walking; a little west of north now, because when we seen his white flag that second or two before the thicket hid it, it was on a beeline for that notch in the bayou. And it was evening, too, now. The wind had done dropped and there was a edge to the air and the sun jest touched the tops of the trees now, except jest now and then, when it found a hole to come almost level through onto the ground. And he was taking the easiest way, too, now, going straight as he could. When we seen his foot in the soft places he was running for a while at first after his rest. But soon he was walking, too, like he knowed, too, where Eagle and the dogs was.

And then we seen him again. It was the last time—a thicket, with the sun coming through a hole onto it like a searchlight. He crashed jest once; then he was standing there broadside to us, not twenty yards away, big as a statue and red as gold in the sun, and the sun sparking on the tips of his horns—they was twelve of them—so that he looked like he had twelve lighted candles branched around his head, standing there looking at us while Mister Ernest raised the gun and aimed at his neck, and the gun went, "Click. Snick-cluck. Click. Snick-cluck. Click. Snick-cluck" three times, and Mister Ernest still holding the gun aimed while the buck turned and give one long bound, the white underside of his tail like a blaze of fire, too, until the thicket and the shadows put it out; and Mister Ernest laid the gun slow and gentle

*A herd of whitetails fords a marsh. (Photo © Leonard Lee Rue III)*

Above: *With his antlers bedecked by a wreath of Spanish moss, a Mississippi whitetail buck reaches to eat from an oak branch. (Photo © Stephen Kirkpatrick)*

Facing page, both photos: *Two large bucks battle for dominance during the rut. (Photos © Jamie Ruggles)*

back across the saddle in front of him, saying quiet and peaceful, and not much louder than jest breathing, "God dawg. God dawg."

Then he jogged me with his elbow and we got down, easy and careful because of that ere cinch strop, and he reached into his vest and taken out one of the cigars. It was busted where I had fell on it, I reckon, when we hit the ground. He throwed it away and taken out the other one. It was busted, too, so he bit off a hunk of it to chew and throwed the rest away. And now the sun was gone even from the tops of the trees and there wasn't nothing left but a big red glare in the west.

"Don't worry," I said. "I ain't going to tell them you forgot to load your gun. For that matter, they don't need to know we ever seed him."

"Much oblige," Mister Ernest said. There wasn't going to be no moon tonight neither, so he taken the compass off the whang leather loop in his buttonhole and handed me the gun and set the compass on a stump and stepped back and looked at it. "Jest about the way we're headed now," he said, and taken the gun from me and opened it and put one shell in the britch and taken up the compass, and I taken Dan's reins and we started, with him in front with the compass in his hand.

And after a while it was full dark; Mister Ernest would have to strike a match ever now and then to read the compass, until the stars come out good and we could pick out one to follow, because I said, "How fur do you reckon it is?" and he said, "A little more than one box of matches." So we used a star when we could, only we couldn't see it all the time because the woods was too dense and we would git a little off until he would have to spend another match. And now it was good and late, and he stopped and said, "Get on the horse."

"I ain't tired," I said.

"Get on the horse," he said. "We don't want to spoil him."

Because he had been a good feller ever since I had knowed him, which was even before that day two years ago when maw went off with the Vicksburg roadhouse feller and the next day pap didn't come home neither, and on the third one Mister Ernest rid Dan up to the door of the cabin on the river he let us live in, so pap could work his piece of land and

run his fish line, too, and said, "Put that gun down and come on here and climb up behind."

So I got in the saddle even if I couldn't reach the stirrups, and Mister Ernest taken the reins and I must 'a' went to sleep, because the next thing I knowed a buttonhole of my lumberjack was tied to the saddle horn with that ere whang cord off the compass, and it was good and late now and we wasn't fur, because Dan was already smelling water, the river. Or maybe it was the feed lot itself he smelled, because we struck the fire road not a quarter below it, and soon I could see the river, too, with the white mist laying on it soft and still as cotton. Then the lot, home; and up yonder in the dark, not no piece akchully, close enough to hear us unsaddling and shucking corn prob'ly, and sholy close enough to hear Mister Ernest blowing his horn at the dark camp for Simon to come in the boat and git us, that old buck in his brake in the bayou; home, too, resting, too, after the hard run, waking hisself now and then, dreaming of dogs behind him or maybe it was the racket we was making would wake him, but not neither of them for more than jest a little while before sleeping again.

Then Mister Ernest stood on the bank blowing until Simon's lantern went bobbing down into the mist; then we clumb down to the landing and Mister Ernest blowed again now and then to guide Simon, until we seen the lantern in the mist, and then Simon and the boat; only it looked like ever time I set down and got still, I went back to sleep, because Mister Ernest was shaking me again to git out and climb the bank into the dark camp, until I felt a bed against my knees and tumbled into it.

Then it was morning, tomorrow; it was all over now until next November, next year, and we could come back. Uncle Ike and Willy and Walter and Roth and the rest of them had come in yestiddy, soon as Eagle taken the buck out of hearing and they knowed that deer was gone, to pack up and be ready to leave this morning for Yoknapatawpha, where they lived, until it would be November again and they could come back again.

So, as soon as we et breakfast, Simon run them back up the river in the big boat to where they left their cars and pickups, and now it wasn't nobody but jest me and Mister Ernest setting on the bench against the kitchen wall in the sun; Mister Ernest

*Whitetail country: Mist rises from a Tennessee stream. (Photo © Jerry and Barbara Jividen/Images Unique)*

smoking a cigar—a whole one this time that Dan hadn't had no chance to jump him through a grapevine and bust. He hadn't washed his face neither where that vine had throwed him into the mud. But that was all right, too; his face usually did have a smudge of mud or tractor grease or beard stubble on it, because he wasn't jest a planter; he was a farmer, he worked as hard as ara one of his hands and tenants—which is why I knowed from the very first that we would git along, that I wouldn't have no trouble with him and he wouldn't have no trouble with me, from that very first day when I woke up and maw had done gone off with that Vicksburg roadhouse feller without even waiting to cook breakfast, and the next morning pap was gone, too, and it was almost night the next day when I heard a horse coming up and I taken the gun that I had already throwed a shell into the britch when pap never come home last night, and stood in the door while Mister Ernest rid up and said, "Come on. Your paw ain't coming back neither."

"You mean he give me to you?" I said.

"Who cares?" he said. "Come on. I brought a lock for the door. We'll send the pickup back tomorrow for what ever you want."

So I come home with him and it was all right, it was jest fine—his wife had died about three years ago—without no women to worry us or take off in the middle of the night with a durn Vicksburg roadhouse jake without even waiting to cook breakfast. And we would go home this afternoon, too, but not jest yet; we always stayed one more day after the others left because Uncle Ike always left what grub they hadn't et, and the rest of the homemade corn whisky he drunk and that town whisky of Roth Edmondziz he called Scotch that smelled like it come out of a old bucket of roof paint; setting in the sun for one more day before we went back home to git ready to put in next year's crop of cotton and oats and beans and hay; and across the river yonder, behind the wall of trees where the big woods started, that old buck laying up today in the sun, too—resting today, too, without nobody to bother him until next November.

So at least one of us was glad it would be eleven

*A buck stands in the warmth of the morning sun. (Photo © Bruce Montagne)*

months and two weeks before he would have to run that fur that fast again. So he was glad of the very same thing we was sorry of, and so all of a sudden I thought about how maybe planting and working and then harvesting oats and cotton and beans and hay wasn't jest something me and Mister Ernest done three hundred and fifty-one days to fill in the time until we could come back hunting again, but it was something we had to do, and do honest and good during the three hundred and fifty-one days, to have the right to come back into the big woods and hunt for the other fourteen; and the fourteen days that old buck run in front of dogs wasn't jest something to fill his time until the three hundred and fifty-one when he didn't have to, but the running and the risking in front of guns and dogs was something he had to do for fourteen days to have the right not to be bothered for the other three hundred and fifty-one. And so the hunting and the farming wasn't two different things atall—they was jest the other side of each other.

"Yes," I said. "All we got to do now is put in that next year's crop. Then November won't be no time away atall."

"You ain't going to put in the crop next year," Mister Ernest said. "You're going to school."

So at first I didn't even believe I had heard him. "What?" I said. "Me? Go to school?"

"Yes," Mister Ernest said. "You must make something out of yourself."

"I am," I said. "I'm doing it now. I'm going to be a hunter and a farmer like you."

"No," Mister Ernest said. "That ain't enough any more. Time was when all a man had to do was just farm eleven and a half months, and hunt the other half. But not now. Now just to belong to the farming business and the hunting business ain't enough. You got to belong to the business of mankind."

"Mankind?" I said.

"Yes," Mister Ernest said. "So you're going to school. Because you got to know why. You can belong to the farming and hunting business and you can learn the difference between what's right and what's wrong, and do right. And that used to be enough—just to do right. But not now. You got to know why it's right and why it's wrong, and be able

to tell the folks that never had no chance to learn it; teach them how to do what's right, not just because they know it's right, but because they know now why it's right because you just showed them, told them, taught them why. So you're going to school."

"It's because you been listening to that durn Will Legate and Walter Ewell!" I said.

"No," Mister Ernest said.

"Yes!" I said. "No wonder you missed that buck yestiddy, taking ideas from the very fellers that let him git away, after me and you had run Dan and the dogs durn night clean to death! Because you never even missed him! You never forgot to load that gun! You had done already unloaded it a purpose! I heard you!"

"All right, all right," Mister Ernest said. "Which would you rather have? His bloody head and hide on the kitchen floor yonder and half his meat in a pickup truck on the way to Yoknapatawpha County, or him with his head and hide and meat still together over yonder in that brake, waiting for next November for us to run him again?"

"And git him, too," I said. "We won't even fool with no Willy Legate and Walter Ewell next time."

"Maybe," Mister Ernest said.

"Yes," I said.

"Maybe," Mister Ernest said. "The best word in our language, the best of all. That's what mankind keeps going on: Maybe. The best days of his life ain't the ones when he said 'Yes' beforehand: they're the ones when all he knew to say was 'Maybe.' He can't say 'Yes' until afterward because he not only don't know it until then, he don't want to know 'Yes' until then. . . . Step in the kitchen and make me a toddy. Then we'll see about dinner."

"All right," I said. I got up. "You want some of Uncle Ike's corn or that town whisky of Roth Edmondziz?"

"Can't you say Mister Roth or Mister Edmonds?" Mister Ernest said.

"Yes, sir," I said. "Well, which do you want? Uncle Ike's corn or that ere stuff of Roth Edmondziz?"

*Standing on her hind legs, a whitetail doe stretches to eat from a cedar tree. (Photo © Bruce Montagne)*

## Chapter 5

# DEER HUNTING
# DAYS GONE BY

*Every year in late September or early October, the funny feeling finds its way
into my body. I wake one day and the summer is over. There is a cool snap to
the air, suddenly the leaves have turned and the wind is pulling them
down. I find a new energy, long dormant with the summer heat, and a
strange sort of nervous excitement lies just beneath the surface of my
day-to-day outward demeanor. It's hunting season.*
—*Jim Rikhoff, "First Buck," 1979*

# LIFE IN WISCONSIN'S OLD-TIME DEER CAMPS

## by Mel Ellis

Mel Ellis had a soft spot in his heart for gun dogs, deer stalking, and the olden days of hunting, as revealed in this tribute to deer camps. For many years Ellis was the dean of outdoors writers for the *Milwaukee Journal,* and his columns and articles were revered by hunters and anglers in Wisconsin. He also authored numerous novels, several of which were made into movies, including *The Wild Horse Killers* and two Disney Studio television films, *Wild Goose, Brother Goose* and *Flight of the White Wolf.* Here is his remembrance of things past.

For more than fifty weeks each year, except for mice in the mattresses and perchance a porcupine in the loft, they are deserted. They almost disappear beneath winter snows when storm upon storm vaults drifts as high as the eaves, and sometimes even higher, until only the chimney, like a blackened eye, stares skyward to mark the place.

Against the fresh bright green of spring they stand starkly weather-beaten until grass stands high enough to hide their shaky foundations and vines climb upward log over log to cover the ax scars. By summer only the shingles are bare to curl in the heat.

The vines wither again, the nights grow cold, there is frost on the stoop and a fringe of ice along the creek, and still no man arrives. But finally one day, to this place where the red squirrel and the woodpecker went their raucous rounds, come men, and for a short ten days or so, the citizens of the wild society stand in awe of these two-legged phenomena.

Most women, of course, call it uncivilized. Men who come to deer camps let their beards grow. They take on a fragrance reminiscent of sweaty hours on the trail. If they clean their fingernails at all, it is with a pine splinter, and hair that gets three licks with a wet palm is considered combed. But uncivilized or not, deer camps are part of Wisconsin's heritage. Unfortunately, however, these hermitages upon which men converge each November and—holding hunting as an excuse—abandon themselves to slovenly living, are disappearing. Where nine out of ten hunters once came to compensate for the more than three hundred fifty days of the year they were required to go properly stuffed in starched shirts, now only a scattering of hardhanded ones still meet.

Pages 150–151: *A whitetail buck with its glorious rack of antlers silhouetted against the sky. (Photo © T. Urban)*

Page 151, inset: *A classic hunting camp of days gone by, this one owned by William Roleff and situated at Gooseberry Crossing in Lake County, Minnesota, in 1916. (Photo by William Roleff, courtesy Minnesota Historical Society)*

Facing page: *An antique deer-huntering rifle from the old country: A Purdey 16-gauge rifle with swivel breech. (Photo © William W. Headrick)*

I've lived in many camps, but somehow, in remembering, they all merge into one Sawyer County cabin. When I sit down to write about a single deer camp, every deer camp I've ever been in crowds around for its full share, so the Sawyer County camp is only a symbol for all the others I've known.

Of all the appurtenances necessary to a deer camp, the beds have fascinated me most. Perhaps it is because each has its own peculiar odor. Sometimes the smell comes from previous occupants—mice or men. Mice, I can tell you, leave a musty odor. With red squirrels, the smell is sharper. And if a grouse has got in through a window broken by a bear, the bed may have a vinegary odor. It depends, too, on the stuffings. I've slept on beds stuffed with pine needles, and so what if they are hard as cement? Just to lie close to the clean smell of resin is reward enough for the lumps. Corn stalks, hay, leaves, straw, cotton, all bring their special dreams. Still, I can recall no deer camp mattress which reminded me of floating on a cloud.

The most illustrious bed of all was a tent bed which somebody said had been in use for fifty years. (I doubt this because it seems the logs would have rotted away.) This bed was enormous, a superbed meant to sleep ten or a dozen or fifteen. It was an oblong structure of ten-inch logs fitted like the foundation of a cabin and rising perhaps four feet. It was some seven feet deep and twice as long, maybe even longer. Each fall the old hay was taken out and burned and nearly a whole rick of new hay was put in. Then a tent large enough to house a small circus was set up over the bed and—presto!—a cozy communal pad. Each member of the hunting party crawled in with the others and curled up like a snake in hibernation to stay warm while the wild wind howled.

The big bed had some drawbacks, though. Since beer was a staple in this Price County camp, many a man got the call and then sleepily had to walk across an entire cluster of companions to reach the tent flap. But I think I know why so much beer was consumed in this camp. It was necessary because no man who came to bed without first having been considerably sedated could come to terms with Morpheus amid all that groaning, talking, kicking, rolling, toss-

ing, snoring, coughing, and wheezing. I don't know what happened to that bed. Perhaps it still accommodates deer stalkers. If it does, and if it could tell its tales, *there* would be a story worth the reading.

But to get back to the Sawyer County camp. It is the camp I think of first when I start remembering the hundreds of times I reveled in going back, at least a little way, toward the days when animal fat lighted the cave of my ancestors. Maybe there was a Mel back then who could live for the minute because if he didn't, there likely would be no tomorrow.

The camp wasn't mine, that is, I didn't own it. It was the property of a conservation warden and stood in a sugar bush near the Chippewa Flowage. It had two rooms. One was lined with bunks and had a table in the center for playing poker. The other had a woodburning range and another table for meals.

Among the deer camps I have been in, it surely was not the most primitive. Some cabins were more than a century old, and not too infrequently, camp was only a lean-to hastily erected to keep the snow off our sleeping bags. But this camp had flavor. Maybe the people who came to it gave it that flavor; maybe it was the people who had come before—the loggers, the syrup makers, the fishermen, the hunters who were already dead when I was born.

Anyway, I could come, even if I'd been away for five years, and before I crossed the threshold I felt at peace with myself and the world. I literally could heave a great sigh as though a burden of physical proportions had been lifted from my back. That was the kind of camp it was, a place that shuts out the world and all the worry that goes with it. It stood in good deer country, but I am sure it would have been the same under the sun of the Sahara or within reach of a high tide.

I will not try to describe the camp in detail; physically it was nondescript. But it engendered a feeling, and that is what makes it important, at least to me. Deer camps are disappearing now—have all but disappeared—but if I can give you a hint of how it was, perhaps you will understand what a deer camp was like, and perhaps they will be important to you, too.

Anyway, this deer camp was a wind howling down the chimney, snow swirling past the windows, trees groaning in the wind, and snow squeaking

*A ten-point buck with a crown of antlers highlighted by the sun. (Photo © Bruce Montagne)*

underfoot along the path to the little two-holer with the sign, "Bear Trap!" This camp was five-pound chunks of American, Swiss, and Cheddar cheese standing on the cutting board, beans browned with sugar and covered with salt pork waiting on the stove. It was rifles standing in a corner, red clothing steaming on chair backs, tiny streams of water running across the floor from boots by the door, gloves drying in an open oven. There was frost creeping up the windowpane, snow piling high around the woodpile, tracks up the trail sifting full and fading. . . .

And here's what I remember.

How Guy claimed he nipped just enough hair off the belly of a buck to tie a streamer fly. There on the table was the twist of hair, and around it we stood, telling Guy he had cut it off a cow.

How the Old Man said his gun jammed when two bucks walked past single file, not twenty feet away. And how we rationed his grog until he promised not to tell tales like that.

How a fawn came right out of the alders and walked up to the youngest member of the hunting party, and after nuzzling his sleeve, turned and raced away.

How a weasel came out of a hole the size of a broomstick in the snow and it looked as if he had a black head. But weasels do not have black heads; it was only a weasel carrying a mole in his mouth.

How the sharp-tailed grouse flew cackling out of the thorn apples and the ruffed grouse shot down from their bedding places in the maples to dive and disappear in the snow.

How Casey came in to tell about a bear den he had found and we all went out to have a look and when Johnny poked around, two porcupines came waddling out.

How burning maple chunks smell, how wet popple smokes, and how the syrup in the whiskey bottle came right out of the sugar bush back of the cabin and the honey in the fruit jar right out of a bee tree just down the logging trail.

How it was thirty degrees below zero on the thermometer that read the same in summer, and how—when a mouse drowned in the water can—Curtis melted snow to drink until a farmer came with his

*Its natural camouflage gone with a snowfall, a Michigan buck watches warily from protective cover. (Photo © Bruce Montagne)*

team and a stone boat and two milk cans with fresh water.

How all the cars were stuck and stayed stuck until the season ended. Then two days were spent shoveling and shoving them out to road.

How a fire crackles, a broom swishes, a clock ticks. How poker chips are scattered across the table, and dirty glasses line the shelves, window sills, and sink board.

How icicles hung down from the eaves in front of the windows, or socks steamed on a line strung across and over the stove, or deer hung stiffly from the meat pole. The leaden sky sagged right down into the trees and the smoke fell flat away from the chimney.

Frozen water pail, frozen windshields, frozen feet. Red noses. Schnapps bottle in the cupboard. Snoring in a corner. These were the signs, the undeniable signs, that this was a deer camp, and here Wisconsin hunters had come to live in grubby but affable intimacy.

**Day was** when there were hundreds and thousands of camps like this, and all were warmed by fires and the banter of men from Argyle and Milwaukee, from Racine and Ashippun, from cities and villages and farms. Once whole tent colonies sprang up in the Price County sheep ranch country and along the fringes of the great forests of Flambeau, Chequamegon, and Nicolet. But now hardly any show up to light the fires. Where fifty tents once sprouted like mushrooms, there may be one or two. Where the smoke came from the chimneys of a thousand cabins, the flames now leap from the hearths of maybe ten or twenty.

It is sad, but not for those who knew the deer camps, who lived in them and loved them. It is sad for the youngsters who will never have a chance to know them.

This wholesale defection from the rugged life can't be blamed entirely on a weakening of the physical fiber of today's deer hunter. Yesterday pines marked an intersection where a motel now sprawls. Signs at resort roads which formerly read "Closed for the Season," now have larger letters reading "Deer Hunters Welcome!"

Even the deer themselves have had a hand in the gradual disappearance of the old-time camp by moving south into marshes and woodlots. Weekend hunters came into being, and it is possible for a man driving home from work in Waukesha County or near Manitowoc or Wautoma to kill a deer before supper.

Many of the camps are deserted all fifty-two weeks of the year now. They are moldering away. But if there is one loss greater than the others, I think it is this. In the old deer camps, thousands upon thousands of busy and harassed men found that by going back to a more primitive life they were able to make a fresh start. They found that breaking ice in the water pail for a drink, chewing coffee grounds left in the bottom of the cup, curling down deep in the blankets to stay warm, bounding across the cold floor to put a match to the kindling, that all these things, and more, in some strange and mysterious way rejuvenated them and gave them the courage they needed to face the civilized life for another year.

*Facing page: Seeking protective cover in farm country, a doe beds down between corn rows. (Photo © Bill Marchel)*
*Overleaf: A Mississippi whitetail buck jumps a barbed-wire fence and dashes away to freedom. (Photo © Stephen Kirkpatrick)*